free *associations*

Psychoanalysis, Groups, Politics, Culture

free associations

Psychoanalysis, Groups, Politics, Culture

Volume 3, Part 4 (Number 28)

'an association in which the free development of each
is the condition of the free development of all'

Free Association Books / London / 1993

Free Associations Volume 3, Part 4 (Number 28)
Published in 1993 by Free Association Books Ltd, 26 Freegrove Road, London N7 9RQ, a company owned jointly by Process Press Ltd and T.E. Brown
Copyright © 1993 by Free Association Books unless otherwise specified
British Library Cataloguing in Publication Data
Free Associations: Psychoanalysis, Groups, Politics, Culture – Volume 3, Part 4 (Number 28)
1. Psychoanalysis—Social Aspects–Periodicals
150.19'5'05   BF175
ISSN 0267 0887

Published quarterly by Free Association Books, 26 Freegrove Road, London N7 9RQ. Tel. (071) 609 5646

Subscriptions: Issues of *Free Associations* are numbered in volumes, one volume comprising four issues per year, starting in 1990. Annual subscriptions may begin with any issue. Rates: individual, £25 for four issues or £42.50 for eight issues (overseas individual: £30 for four issues or £50 for eight issues); institutional, £50 for four issues (overseas institutional: £60 for four issues); single copies are £7.50 individual, £10.75 institutional. All prices include postage (but air mail is £10 extra). Order from *Free Associations*, c/o Bailey Management Services, 127 Sandgate Road, Folkestone, Kent CT20 2BL. Payment should be in sterling or US dollars or by credit card (Visa/Barclaycard/MasterCard/Access/American Express). If payment is made in another currency, add the equivalent of £3 to cover bank charges for conversion. Credit card orders can be telephoned to 0303 850501.

North America: *Free Associations* is published in co-operation with Guilford Publications, Inc. Issues are numbered in volumes, one volume comprising four issues, starting in 1990. Subscriptions may begin with any issue. Rates: $30 individual USA, $45 individual Canada/Mexico; $65 institutional USA, $80 institutional Canada/Mexico. All prices include postage. Order from Guilford Publications, Inc., 72 Spring Street, New York, NY 10012, USA. Tel: (212) 431–9800; (800) 365–7006; fax (212) 966–6708. Payment should be in US dollars or by credit card (American Express/MasterCard/Visa).

Indexed in Sociological Abstracts.

Trade distribution for Free Association Books is handled by:
Great Britain: Tiptree Book Services Ltd, Church Road, Tiptree, Colchester, Essex CO5 0SR. Tel. (0621) 819600.
North America: Guilford Publications, Inc., 72 Spring Street, New York, NY 10012. Tel. (212) 431–9800.
Australasia: ASTAM Books, 162/168 Parramatta Road, Stanmore, NSW 2048. Tel. (02) 550 3855.
Japan: Far Eastern Book-Sellers, Kanda PO Box No. 72, Tokyo, 101–91. Tel. (03) 265 7531.

Typeset by M.C. Typeset Ltd, Wouldham, Rochester, Kent
Printed in Great Britain

CONTENTS

Editorial

In the history of psychoanalysis, crucial issues which started life in the context of debate often subsequently gave rise to violent schisms and expulsions from the International Psychoanalytical Association. Sadly, such schisms and expulsions also tended to foster narrow introspection within analytic institutions, and unchallenged traditions were established about what should or should not be read: Freudians, for example, read little Jung and Jungians read little Freud.

It has always been one of the principal aims of *Free Associations* to inform readers about the variety of and difference between psychoanalytic perspectives, and to encourage debate across traditional divides. In this issue, we first report on psychoanalysis in Germany. We feature the work of Helmut Dahmer, the editor of *Psyche*, the main German psychoanalytic journal since World War Two. In an interview with Martin Stanton, Dahmer discusses the 'de-realization' of the Nazi period post–1945 and psychoanalytic approaches to this; he also extends this analysis to responses to the unification of East and West Germany.

We also publish a previously untranslated article by Dahmer on the importance of social research in German psychoanalytic work, and a report by Evelyn Heintges on the recent dissolution of *Psyche*, which has shocked the German psychoanalytic community. To complement this, we include a paper by Anthony Elliott which discusses several of the key psycho-social concepts worked out by two of the leading lights of the Frankfurt School – Herbert Marcuse and Theodor Adorno – and critically assesses their implications for the analysis of subjectivity, the unconscious and social relations.

Although the split between Freud and Jung may traditionally be viewed as terminal, such traditions certainly do not apply to all contemporary Freudians and Jungians. In Britain, discussion and debate between Freudians and Jungians were fostered by Donald Winnicott and Michael Fordham, who have left a legacy of open dialogue and eclectic innovation utilizing various psychoanalytic approaches. In this spirit, we asked Andrew Samuels, an eminent Jungian training analyst at the Society of Analytical Psychology, to present a paper on his current views on a major issue in psychoanalysis; and then invited members of Jungian and other psychoanalytic communities to comment. We publish the result here, along with Andrew Samuels' reply to the comments, and hope that this will stimulate further debate among our readers. We intend to continue to stage such debates and would welcome readers' ideas about future topics and participants.

Finally, to complement this debate, we add two articles that dwell on Jung's relationship to psychoanalysis: Michael Fordham writes from his unique experience of the British 'Jung–Klein hybrid', and Margaret Arden contemplates the value of certain critical developments in Jungian thought for Freudian-inspired psychoanalysis.

FEATURE: GERMAN PSYCHOANALYSIS

Interview: Helmut Dahmer talks to Martin Stanton

This interview was conducted in German in Frankfurt on 5 December 1990. The translation is by the interviewer.

Martin Stanton (MS): First of all, I would like to ask you some questions about your own contributions to psychoanalysis in Germany. You are well known in Germany for a whole range of things: first, for your publications, especially the immensely influential *Libido und Gesellschaft* (1973), which examines the relationship between psychoanalysis and radical left-wing politics; also as editor for years now of the journal *Psyche*; finally, you've been closely associated with the development of psychoanalytic social research in Germany, which led among other things to the foundation of the Hamburg *Institut für Sozialforschung*. It would be very useful for an English-speaking audience if you could say something about the historical background to this; also your own sense of historical precedents, as you've been very involved in reassessing the role of Siegfried Bernfeld and Wilhelm Reich in the development of German psychoanalysis.

Helmut Dahmer (HD): I began to study these things in the 1950s.

Free Associations (1993) Volume 3, Part 4 (No. 28): 483–89

The first international political event that prompted me to think about these things was the Algerian revolt. In 1954, the German army was recreated and Germany was remilitarized, and I joined the protest against this. Then in 1956 I joined the thousands who protested over the Soviet invasion of Hungary. From 1961 on, I was active in student protest movements that emerged in Germany. I started literary studies in Bonn and in Göttingen; then in Göttingen, and later in Frankfurt, I studied a combination of sociology, philosophy, and political science.

Reading literary figures like Karl Kraus and philosophers like Herbert Marcuse led me to Frankfurt. In Frankfurt, my ideas became oriented around the work of Max Horkheimer, Marcuse, and then later, after 1964, around the work of Jürgen Habermas. My reading of Freud related to those contemporary readings: to Horkheimer's reading of Freud, and the different reading by Adorno. Freud was centrally important for both Adorno and Horkheimer, but in different ways. Adorno taught us that psychoanalytic theory was central for sociology.

The Jewish refugees who returned to Germany after World War Two were a different influence on me at this time. They brought to student groups in Frankfurt insights from their work in Trotskyist groups, and from new social experiments like the *kibbutzim* in Israel where they had spent the war. In their libraries, for example, I came across all the old political publications of Wilhelm Reich for the first time, and started to study him seriously – this, of course, is one way that Reich's ideas became very important for the student movement in the 1960s.

This led me, anyway, to look at the statements about the relationship between the individual and society proposed by the Freudian Left, which, besides Reich, included Bernfeld and Fenichel. So my book *Libido und Gesellschaft* was built around my research on this theme, and stemmed from both Frankfurt critical theory readings of Freud and the writings of the German Freudian Left – very different influences.

MS: What sort of role did Alexander Mitscherlich play in this? Do you regard him as part of the Frankfurt School, or as part of the Freudian Left, or both?

HD: I think that Mitscherlich looked in on the Frankfurt School from the outside. They were friendly neighbours. Mitscherlich was good friends with both Horkheimer and Adorno. There was a sort of coalition between those who returned home after the twelve years of Nazi dictatorship – a coalition built around respect for the importance of Freud in helping understand what had happened. This is what bracketed them together in post-war German politics, and was also one of the things that linked them together in support of the student movement in the 1960s. But one must say that, despite being in the same 'stew', there was no real communication between the Frankfurt School – that is, the Frankfurt Institute for Social Research – and Alexander Mitscherlich's institutions: the Frankfurt Sigmund Freud Institute and the review *Psyche*. This has been especially true for the last fifteen years or so.[1]

MS: That's very interesting, because there is no sense of this outside Germany. One assumes a natural cohesion and sense of common purpose. What about the notion of psychoanalytic sociology then? Does this have any cohesion – even in the sense of being a defined subject area in academic life?

HD: Well, there's been a longstanding concern with Freud among social psychologists in Germany, as represented notably in the work of Kurt Lewin.[2] But as far as psychoanalytic sociology is concerned, the term comes from a title of Erich Fromm's – from a 1932 essay.[3] I think what is interesting in the themes and concerns of psychoanalytic sociology has been the attention to what actually engendered the situation which tore analysts and intellectuals from their mother-earth [*Mutterboden*] – analysts who were ripped from the Vienna–Berlin axis of the German cultural world. Indeed, I would go so far as to say that analytical sociology is the product of German, Jewish psychoanalytically-oriented exiles who lived through that dreadful catastrophe.

In this, it is hard to see some clear critical method in this work, since it relates to people looking back and trying to make sense of their own extraordinary experience. Indeed, the 'beginnings' of analytical sociology lie in personal attempts to deal with this catastrophe, as in Fromm's essays from this period, Paul Federn's *Die Vaterlose Gesellschaft* [*The Fatherless Society*] (1919), Wilhelm

Reich's *The Mass Psychology of Fascism* (1946), and Adorno *et al. The Authoritarian Personality* (1950). In an important way, these are all isolated studies which none the less illustrate the special qualities that psychoanalysis can bring to social research. They have inspired more recent qualitative psychoanalytic social research projects, too, such as those carried out by the Hamburg Institute for Social Research; and those of my friend Rodriguez-Rabanal, who is working in the slums of Lima; and finally those of the Zürich School such as Paul Parin. So now over the last years in Germany there's been more co-ordinated work in psychoanalytic sociology, centred around these groups in Hamburg, Hanover, here in Frankfurt, and Zürich.

MS: You've talked about the 'conformist erosion' of Freud's critical theory. Do you see one of the functions of psychoanalytic sociology as being to counteract that?

HD: Exactly. The problem is that some have construed the therapeutic application of psychoanalysis as the 'pure' one, which has led to an enormous narrowing of horizons. This totally denies the important psychoanalytic work in the 1920s and 1930s on cultural theory: *Totem and Taboo, Civilization and Its Discontents, The Future of an Illusion, Moses and Monotheism*, etc. For some 'pure' analysts, it is as if Freud never wrote these works. In fact, without this cultural impulse, psychoanalytic therapy would not have developed at all. Freud did not stay fixed in the tracks set out by Brücke.[4] But institutional psychoanalysis has ignored this cultural impulse, and its commitment simply to therapeutic technique – that is, its apoliticism – actually supports the political *status quo*.

MS: Do you think it's possible or easy for left-wing or radical psychoanalysts to train in Germany? What sort of obstacles might they meet?

HD: There are two possibilities. The first is for institutionalized psychoanalysts to get involved in interdisciplinary projects, so that they will be obliged to look at other perspectives engendered by the research itself. They will then become integrated in more radical projects. Alternatively, here in Frankfurt – as elsewhere – we are looking at the whole category of 'research psychoanalyst'. This means that psychoanalytic training does not have to be exclusively or even principally therapeutic. This means that the training can be reconciled more readily with group, social, and literary research, etc. Unfortunately, all this proceeds very slowly here . . . This is very much what PSZ – Zürich Psychoanalytic Seminar – has fought for, against, one should say, much diffidence[5] . . . Here in Germany we have a similar project with the Bernfeld Group, which also aims for an integration of psychoanalysis in wider research and interdisciplinary work. These organizations really check the 'conformist erosion' of psychoanalytic theory you mentioned earlier – certainly the erosion enacted in the name of psychoanalytic 'cure'. Instead, they propose through independent research to challenge and disentangle the major riddles [*Rätseln*] of our time. This brings in a sort of relativism – it relativizes clinical work – and makes personal research a more open-ended project.

MS: Finally, I'd like to ask you a few questions about what you call the German 'collective de-realization of the Nazi era' – including the psychoanalytic participation in this 'de-realization'. I think here of your work on Carl Müller-Braunschweig.[6] And, in this context, it seems to me that German 'unification' provides an opportunity critically to extend this category of 'de-realization' in the declaration of the so-called 'end' of the post-war era . . .

HD: As far as Müller-Braunschweig was concerned – I was not personally concerned with him, but with psychoanalytic conformism, the narrowing of psychoanalytic horizons to the political 'norms' of the Nazi period, or the limiting of psychoanalytic critique . . . As far as 'de-realization' is concerned – now there's a basic question here, which has been raised yet again by the Kurt Waldheim affair in Austria:[7] when people 'forget' their actions during the Nazi era, is this simply a lie, or is it 'repression' in the clinical sense? Alexander Mitscherlich elaborated on this question in his original definition of 'realization' and 'de-realization' in *Die Unfähigkeit zu Trauern* [*The Incapacity to Mourn*] (1967).[8]

In this context, it's interesting to observe the antisemitic potential which surfaced in the Waldheim affair. A similar kind of potential exists in East Germany, where for years the people have been dissociated from the Nazi era . . . This was reinforced by the occupation by Soviet troops, who acted, as it were, as a protection against a direct relation to the Nazi era . . . In West Germany it was different: the younger generation reacted against older generations who were actively involved in Nazi policies, especially in the student movement in the 1960s.

Mitscherlich's work on de-realization fitted very much into that context – but there was neither a strong student movement nor a text like Mitscherlich's in East Germany. Instead, there was a Stalinist majority that installed a de-realization of its own. Indeed, the right-wing, the Christian Democrats in West Germany, tried to associate Mitscherlich with Stalinism, and then with the terrorists, which, of course, was absurd. But such absurdities feed the latent aspects of the authoritarian personality which we now see revealed in the so-called new era of German 'unity', notably in the new emergent Right with its familiar antisemitic themes and hostility to foreigners . . .

MS: Many thanks for your time!

HD: My pleasure!

NOTES

1   Despite this, one should mention that Jürgen Habermas was a member of the editorial advisory board of *Psyche* up to its dissolution in 1992.

2   Kurt Lewin fled Germany in 1933 to avoid persecution as a Jew, and settled in the United States. However, his work on the psychology of institutions (which made many references to Freud) became very important in post–1945 Germany (cf. 'The life and work of Kurt Lewin', in de Board, 1978, pp. 49–64).

3   'Über Methode und Aufgabe einer analytischen Sozialpsychologie' (1932), translated as 'The method and function of an analytic social psychology', in Fromm, 1970, pp. 138–62.

4   Ernst Brücke (1819–1892) was one of Freud's first teachers and mentors in phsysiology. He rejected all forms of vitalism and aspired to reduce all psychological processes to physiological laws.

5   The Zürich Psychoanalytical Seminar has pioneered new forms of research co-operation and training. See Modena, 1986.

6 Dahmer, 'Kapitulation vor der "Weltanschauung": zu einem Aufsatz von Carl Müller-Braunschweig aus dem Herbst 1933', in Dahmer, 1989, pp. 145–72. Müller-Braunschweig was one of the major figures in early German psychoanalysis who initially supported the Nazi movement – a fact that has since been largely overlooked.

7 Kurt Waldheim, President of Austria, was accused of being involved in Nazi atrocities in Yugoslavia. He denied all knowledge of this but, when confronted with documentary evidence to the contrary, claimed that he had 'forgotten' all about it.

8 'Techniken der Entwirklichung', in Mitscherlich, 1967, pp. 44–50.

REFERENCES

Adorno, T.W., Frenkel-Brunswik, E., Levinson, D. and Nevitt Sanford, R. (1950) *The Authoritarian Personality*. New York: Norton.

de Board, R. (1978) *The Psychoanalysis of Organizations*. London: Tavistock.

Dahmer, H. (1973) *Libido und Gesellschaft: Studien über Freud und die Freudsche Linke*. Frankfurt: Suhrkamp, 1982.

——— (ed.) (1980) *Analytische Sozialpsychologie*, 2 vols. Frankfurt: Suhrkamp.

——— (1989) *Psychoanalyse ohne Grenzen*. Freiburg: Kore.

Federn, P. (1919) *Die Vaterlose Gesellschaft*. Vienna: Heller.

Fromm, E. (1970) *The Crisis of Psychoanalysis*. New York: Basic.

Mitscherlich, A. and M. (1967) *Die Unfähigkeit zu trauern*. Munich: Piper, 1973.

Modena, E. (1986) 'A chance for psychoanalysis to change: the Zürich Psychoanalytical Seminar as an example', *Free Associations* 5: 7–22.

Reich, W. (1946) *The Mass Psychology of Fascism*. New York: Orgone Institute Press.

Address for correspondence: Centre for Psychoanalytic Studies, Eliot College, The University, Canterbury, Kent CT2 7NS, UK

Psychoanalytic social research

Helmut Dahmer

I

Critical social research has to do with life-threatening or sphinx riddles. The results of our practice, that is, in the formation of institutions of life and social history, become enigmatic because of the lack of consciousness of their production.

Due to the forgetting of their authorship – and bearership – such institutions appear to be 'natural', to be out of our control and beyond any possibility of revision. The unconscious upbringing of such institutions leads to a more and more autonomous life separate from their creators, so that their well-being and woe seem to depend on the institutions alone; and the cult that comes into existence around such institutions is called 'fetishizing' in ethnology, psychology and sociology.

Attempts to puzzle out this puzzle, to defetishize the fetishes and overcome adherence to the fetish cult, cause their supporters mortal danger because the cult blocks the search for alternative ways out of a crisis.

We call these attempts to solve a riddle 'critique'. Examples of such a critique are Marx's solutions of the riddle of capital; Freud's puzzling out of the riddle of hysteria; Trotsky's solution of the riddle of the Soviet Thermidor (and the 'Moscow Trials' which

Translated by Evelyn Heintges and Rita von Schwartzenberg

crowned him); Adorno's illumination of the foundations of anti-semitism, or Alexander and Margaret Mitscherlich's solution to the riddle of the collective amnesia in post-war West Germany. The conceptual instruments of defetishizing critique were developed by Fichte, Schelling and Hegel in respect of the riddle of the French Revolution in the form of a dialectic of alienation and reappropriation. Marx, as much as Freud, modified this critical dialectic for his own purposes. However, the mythical model for all riddle solvers is Oedipus, who solved the riddle asked by the Sphinx intuitively (or 'hermeneutically'), whereas he solved that of the Laius-murderer like a detective.

Actually, we have to deal with two versions of the same riddle: the confrontation with the Sphinx (and her question), and the search for the Laius-murderer as a self-confrontation.

Oedipus, deprived of his identity because his parents exposed him, and threatened with a divine curse, is as much the classic unconscious committer of a crime as one who breaks the law through the lack of consciousness that has been imposed on him: that is, the first 'critic'. Even the crossing of 'explaining' and 'understanding', which has been understood as specific to the 'critique of ideology', is preformed in Sophocles' *Oedipus Rex*.

II

At the 'end of the soul' of the modern world, Freud, a modern Oedipus, saw himself as being confronted with the double riddle of hysteria and dream. By self-analysis he deciphered the first as the prototype of an until-then unknown genus of 'social suffering' (Ferenczi), and the latter as rendered unrecognizable through 'censorship', alienated but principally an understandable product of the 'normal' work of the psyche. To be able to understand the unintelligible, Freud provoked his clients to so-called 'free associations' and used this spontaneous train of thought on ego-alienated symptoms and nonsensical dream-fragments as a trace from which the secret life-circumstances of dreamers and hysterics could be inferred. The therapy leads to a reconstruction of the traumas and crises of his or her life, to exactly the same degree as detective-like interpretations become acceptable for the analysand.

Thus a revelation of forgotten authorship also takes place and that means self-confrontation.

Hysterics, like dreamers, have lost themselves. They do not realize that their productions belong to them, nor do they realize themselves as taking part in them.

The therapeutic reconstruction of many life stories of hysterics, men and women, gave Freud a gradual understanding of the aetiology of neurosis. In a conflict situation accumulated traumas leave the weakened ego only the possibility of self-resignation to master them. Then the conflict is repressed, split off and 'fetishized'; but the further life of the neurotic is unrecognizably, completely spellbound by the 'fetish'.

What has once been left undigested, and has led to a split of the ego, becomes immortal by repression. The patient stages an eternal repetition of the same thing. He is permanently wrestling with the old traumas which continually renew themselves. Again and again he reproduces the long-institutionalized defence which has once been improvised in panic and distress.

The therapy uses free association to break this compulsion to repeat, and clears the way for anamnesis with the help of interpretations. The deficit of neurosis consists in the fact that one does not understand oneself (anymore) and fancies oneself as being 'overcome' by ego-alien symptoms. The neurotic not-knowing-anymore is conditioned by social taboos and is produced by individual censorship.

The social norms of feeling, thinking and acting are altogether taboo regulations. Their essence, the 'reality principle', is the fetish. This is the truth in Émile Durkheim's thesis that every society is first of all a 'morally' joined community of compulsion. Freud reads history as the cumulative process of renunciation of fulfilments of drives, which is imposed on a reluctant majority by the ruling privileged minority. He thinks that considering the social riches achieved by the work of many generations, the traditional form of socialization in which the majority is exploited and forced into superstition, becomes obsolete. Hence derives the spreading 'uneasiness in culture'[1] helplessly demonstrated by the neurotic. The oedipal conflict is constituent for the biography of the individual because it leads to the breaking of the first drive wishes, which are bound to other people. Thus it enables their identification with the machinery of collective self-preservation. The socializing superposition of the social reality principle above the 'pleasure principle' leads to a taboo on individual experience and reflection. Such a taboo removes an essential part of the individual and collective practice from consciousness (which is bound to language). What is withdrawn in that way from the consciousness of the socialized individual is ruled by the taboo with the power of nature. The internalized rules of taboo secure the everyday routine of class societies. The class individuals, in the course of their socialization, appropriate the culture of suppression to themselves and become its reluctant unconscious carriers.

Acculturation produces in the socialized individuals a relation, at any time precarious, between accepted losses and real satisfactions that are within reach, and imaginary compensations (type: religion); this is modulated according to social position. The social fights for change of the 'reality principle', the means for a shifting of socially defined borders between 'possible' and 'impossible', are reflected within the social monads as the conflict between the conformist and rebellious impulses. It is a conflict which cannot be mediated between the wish to secure their lives by adjustment to the socially acceptable pattern of life and experience and the contrary, which is to change their lives by experiments with innovation and by the search for alternatives. Individuals have command neither of their individuality nor of the collective practice in which they are involved. They are therefore dominated by circumstances which they themselves again produce. They do not know (enough) what they are doing; all the same they talk about it yet without knowing what they are saying. This double incongruity gives us, as a result, the need for 'interpretation' and the possibility of 'critique'. The target of both of them is to bring into consciousness life – and socio-historically produced preconditions and borders of practice to cast off their pretension to be natural; that means to enable them to be revised. The predominant *status quo* of a society and the kind of accommodated individual lifestyle are fixed by institutionalized taboo-borders.

Wherever such a 'censorship' is loosened the surplus potential of the socialized finds its expression in 'free association', those despised ideas [*Einfälle*] out of which the innovations in thinking and practice derive.

The psychoanalytic cure is an arrangement in order to lower the censorship that holds the individuals in check. In the therapeutic dialogue the surplus of an otherwise tabooed self- and social experience can be articulated because it is set free by the reduction of inhibitions. Out of this surplus, the code for an understanding of the symptom-fetishes that dominate the patient can be revealed, and this code deciphers their lost meaning.

III

For Freud the 'psyche' is a *Reizbewältigungsapparat*, a mechanism to cope with stimuli that works with symbolizations and puts self- and world-experience in metaphors, and that functions mainly unconsciously. Therapy of hysteria and dream interpretation forced Freud to distinguish two overlapping psychic processes: the 'primary process', in which the stream of imaginings follows changing drive impulses (and the tendency to avoid unpleasure); and the 'secondary process', which subjugates this pleasurable chaotic 'stream of consciousness' to the programme of self-preservation in an unpleasurable socially-defined reality, which inhibits its (purpose-)free movement, states identities and introduces negations:

As a result of the unpleasure principle, then, the first psychic system is totally incapable of bringing anything disagreeable into the context of its thoughts. It is unable to do anything but wish. If things remained at that point, the thought-activity of the second system would be obstructed, since it requires free access to *all* the memories laid down by experience.

Accordingly, thinking must aim at freeing itself more and more from exclusive regulation by the unpleasure principle and at restricting the development of affect in thought-activity to the minimum required for acting as a signal. The achievement of this greater delicacy in functioning is aimed at by means of a further hypercathexis, brought about by consciousness. As we well know, however, that aim is seldom attained completely, even in normal mental life, and our thinking always remains exposed to falsification by interference from the unpleasure principle.

It is true that, so far as we know, no psychical apparatus exists which possesses a primary process only and that such an apparatus is to that extent a theoretical fiction. But this much is a fact: the primary processes are present in the mental apparatus from the first, while it is only during the course of life that the secondary processes unfold, and come to inhibit and overlay the primary ones; it may even be that their complete domination is not attained until the prime of life. In consequence of the belated appearance of the secondary processes, the core of our being, consisting of unconscious wishful impulses, remains inaccessible to the understanding and inhibition of the preconscious; the part played by the latter is restricted once and for all to directing along the most expedient paths the wishful impulses that arise from the unconscious. (1990, pp. 600–603)[2]

The 'ego' is situated on the 'outer skin' of the psyche, where the soul touches the world. It is considered as a surface-being that is stamped by the 'outer reality', and actually even belongs to it. The ego-authority, in which the faculty of speech is developed during the process of early socialization and to which therefore consciousness is linked, 'examines' reality in the interest of self-preservation (and of a wish-fulfilment which colludes with self-preservation). The ego-authority is the organ of realizing oneself and the world, but also reaches into the unconscious past of the psyche where social regulations, taboos and ideals of renunciation are deposited. Therefore the ego is not only an organ of cognition, but at the same time a censorship authority, and arsenal of the defence mechanisms. All recognition of reality must first be wrested from the primary process. And the image that we create of the world and ourselves is always in danger of becoming falsified and simplified through our desires and anxieties.

The interference of primary and secondary processes is the

source of lively, differentiated experience as well as of its decay: the regression to illusions and clichés. Concerning the world of politics, the average disposable capacities of learning, processing of information and judgement have obviously lagged far behind the increasing importance of 'politics' for everyday life and the profusion of political information. Also, it is true that the majority of people living in highly developed societies actually do not live in the present and do not know the structure and dynamics of the society in which their lives take place. Political learning and operating, quite apart from work and recreation, need free time and energy. As long as the majority cannot cope with politics and do not spend time on it, all politics remain substitute politics. Time is still limited, so that in the daily routine of society participation is 'utopia'. Politics appear abstract but also highly relevant; they seem far away from personal experience but at the same time decisive for one's own life. Political reality, therefore, unlike most of the manifold realities of life, undergoes a radical reduction of complexity. Under the pressure of commanding individual and collective needs political reality is translated into the pseudo-concrete mythology of political world images – spontaneously by everyone, professionally by representatives of the political caste and by the mass media.

The importance of *The Authoritarian Personality* is above all due to the fact that it was possible for the authors, with the help of their own invented assessment scales, to describe for the first time how politics are experienced by (rather prejudiced and rather unprejudiced) contemporaries (Adorno *et al.*, 1950). This means that functions fall to specific political power constellations, institutions and programmes according to the soul – and world view – organization of different individuals. Explanations aimed at a layer of personal structure, called 'mentality', 'disposition' or 'character', involve pre-decisions which are made, based on and depend on the life history and political options, actions or apathy of individuals. According to the mode of interpretation – which is defined by the character, disposition, and according to the political power relation of conforming and revolutionary impulses – current political matters are translated into a primitive relation of good and evil.

Therefore the sphere of political experience is a realm of projections. With the means of transformation which are characteristic of the primary process (condensations and displacements of different size and importance) groups become dominated by prejudices and superstitution and create political-psychological arcane languages.

An example of this is the disreputable, antisemitic *Welterklärungs-formel* that has started to appear again in recent years as graffiti in our cities: $ + $\mathbf{\Delta}$ = $\mathbf{\hat{\varphi}}$· [dollar + hammer and sickle = star of David]. Put into words, this symbolic equation expresses something like: 'Plutocracy and Bolshevism are agencies of the Jewish world-conspiracy'. In short: 'The Jews are our misfortune'. It becomes clear that in slogans of this kind, arcane language functions as a key. In order to set free a suppressed malice, they focus the hatred of underprivileged individuals onto designated groups. Scapegoats and victims arouse a willingness to act on a corresponding political signal. The equation of the dollar symbol, hammer and sickle and the Jewish star belongs to the genre of those sphinx riddles whose solving needs psychoanalytic social research.

IV

The use of psychoanalysis in social research has so far been limited to psychoanalytic interpretations of interview records or literary texts. Only in the best cases has the intention (psychoanalytic interpretation) also affected the mode of production of the text ('open', 'narrative' or 'depth interviews'). This applies to *The Authoritarian Personality*, in which Adorno says:

> It would go beyond the scope of the present study to attempt a full explanation of political ignorance so strikingly in contrast to the level of information in many other matters and to the highly rational way in which most of our subjects decide about the means and ends of their own lives.
>
> To sum up, political ignorance would seem to be specifically determined by the fact that political knowledge as a rule does not primarily help to further individual aims in reality, whereas, on the other hand, it does not help the individual to evade reality either. (1950, pp. 661)

It also applies to the studies of Thomas Leithäuser and his fellow researchers in the 1980s. In the case of the non-pathographically-oriented psychoanalytic interpretation of literary texts, as was developed by Alfred Lorenzer (1986, pp. 11–98), the therapeutic dialogue is simulated: the reader interprets the text with the help of his own free associations; the text and the group have controlling functions in this kind of interpretation.

An alternative to these ways of using psychoanalysis in social research has been developed by 'ethno-psychoanalysts' (Parin, Morgenthaler, Erdheim and Nadig). They not only consult psychoanalysis for interpretation of the text, but involve psychoanalysis in its production. The psychoanalytic procedure of provoking 'free associations' which go beyond the manifest statements of one partner in a dialogue is here used outside the therapeutic setting in order to solve the riddle or enigma of an unfamiliar form of living, with the help of information given by a member of this culture. Using the psychoanalytic procedure of explanation non-therapeutically in this way, the social frame of life histories, and the role which social institutions and political events play in the consciousnes and unconsciousness of the client, become important subject matter.

The experimental return of ethno-psychoanalysis to the culture of the researcher, an attempt at ethno-psychoanalysis in one's home country, has not yet been undertaken. However, a step in this direction is the project of a group of Peruvian ethno-psychoanalysts gathered around César Rodriguez-Rabanal who try to extract from psychoanalytic dialogues a portrait of the way of life and *Weltanschauung* of those members of the Indian majority of the populations who left the Andes and ended up in the slums of Lima. Ethno-psychoanalytic research results, just as in psychoanalytic 'case histories', in illumination of the ways in which social institutions and political events are mirrored in the conscious and unconscious experience of individual members and contemporaries, and in which they entangle with the aim of their drives. The risk of psychologistic misinterpretation, in the reconstruction of social environments with the help of informative dialogues, can only be avoided through educating ethno-psychoanalytic field researchers in psychoanalysis as well as in sociology. For history is always the history of the modes of production and of the soul. Therefore the social world can only be sufficiently understood in a utraquistic way (Ferenczi)[3] – i.e., through the interaction of social and psychological perspectives which inflect one another.

NOTES

1 Translators' note: This would be the literal translation of the title of Freud's book *Das Unbehagen in der Kultur*, usually rendered as *Civilization and Its Discontents*.

2 Translators' note: Freud quotations in this article are translated directly from the German *Gesammelte Werke*.

3 'Utraquism' was the name Ferenczi gave to his theory of analogies (Ferenczi, 1926, p. 373; Stanton, 1991, pp. 64ff., p. 200).

REFERENCES

Adorno, T.W., Frenkel-Brunswik, E., Levinson, D. and Nevitt Sanford, R. (1950) *The Authoritarian Personality*. New York: Norton.

Ferenczi, S. (1926) 'The problem of acceptance of unpleasant ideas – advances in knowledge of the sense of reality', in *Further Contributions to the Theory and Technique of Psychoanalysis*. London: Maresfield.

Freud, S. (1900) *Die Traumdeutung*. Frankfurt: Fischer.

Lorenzer, A. (1986) 'Tiefenhermeneutische Kulturanalyse', *Kultur-Analysen*. Frankfurt: Suhrkamp.

Stanton, M., (1991) *Sandor Ferenczi: Reconsidering Active Intervention*. London: Free Association Books.

Address for correspondence: Institut für Soziologie, Fachbereich 2, Technische Hochschule Darmstadt, 6100 Darmstadt, Residenzschloss, Germany

Report: What caused the disappearance of *Psyche*?

Evelyn Heintges

The renowned Frankfurt psychoanalytic journal *Psyche* does not exist anymore. But maybe its subscribers will not notice this because they have received, without any transition, a journal which has a similar cover and layout. Whether its content is similar remains to be seen. However, there is a difference in the title: this new journal is called *Psychoanalyse – Klinik und Kulturkritic* [*Psychoanalysis – Clinical and Cultural Criticism*]. Readers who may be startled by this may calm down when they read vol. 46, issue 2, and then they may well think that this is, after all, just a continuation of *Psyche*. But as Helmut Dahmer, one of the well-known editors of *Psyche*, sees it, the subscribers have every reason to be shocked, because behind this enigmatic change of the title lies a fully-fledged scandal. If he/she is attentive, the reader will note the name of Margarete Mitscherlich as editor. The names of Helmut Dahmer and Lutz Rosenkötter are omitted. What has happened?

Margarete Mitscherlich, widow of the celebrated Alexander Mitscherlich, left the editorial board of *Psyche* on 13 December 1991. Shortly after that she published, together with a couple of former editorial consultants, a press statement which accused the 'Dahmer Group' of ruining *Psyche*. She had apparently joined

Free Associations (1993) Volume 3, Part 4 (No. 28): 500–502

forces with *Psyche*'s publishing house, Klett/Cotta, which had already given notice that it would terminate all of *Psyche*'s contracts. Mrs Mitscherlich became the only editor of the new journal, which took over the card index of *Psyche* subscribers. The publishing house has refused Helmut Dahmer and Lutz Rosenkötter access to it, which was one of the main reasons why they could not find another publishing house for *Psyche*.

The copyright for the title *Psyche*, by the way, does not belong to Klett/Cotta but to the three former editors. For several months Dahmer and Rosenkötter therefore tried to save *Psyche* by publishing appeals for donations in order to finance the conflict with Klett/Cotta and Mitscherlich. But after a judicial decision by the Frankfurter Landesgericht on 5 February 1992, which entitles the publishing house to do with the enterprise *Psyche* whatever they want to, the three decided, at the end of February, to give up the fight.

To understand the reasons for the whole conflict it is helpful to look at *Psyche*'s history. Alexander Mitscherlich, together with two colleagues, founded the journal in 1947. He had in mind a kind of successor journal to Freud's own periodical *Imago*. His longterm plan was to write about Freudian psychoanalysis not only as a clinical system, but also as a cultural theory and a diagnosis of the *Zeitgeist*. In 1968 Mitscherlich entrusted the post of chief editor to Dahmer, who was editor from 1982, together with Margarete Mitscherlich and Lutz Rosenkötter. Through the years, Dahmer's name became inseparable from *Psyche*, which had been the only monthly German psychoanalytic periodical ever, and remained extraordinarily successful, even after forty-six years. What happens now, or even more what has already happened, has a lot to do with Alexander Mitscherlich's legacy and the surrounding power conflict. According to Dahmer, Margarete Mitscherlich wanted to change *Psyche* in accordance with her own conception of how to run it. She had already been imposing her own ideas for a couple of years by trying, for instance, to appoint her own favoured candidates to posts. Dahmer denies, however, that there had been any essential technical-professional disagreements, as she had stated. Thomas Mitscherlich, Margarete's stepson, suggests that Margarete made a mistake in regarding the journal as her personal heritage. He and Dahmer want to see it belonging to the public.

At the moment it is hard to distinguish objective arguments from polemic derived from bitterness. Nevertheless, it seems more than sad that Margarete Mitscherlich apparently could not see any other way to realize her own ideas; it is also sad that these three unusual and highly competent people could not come to terms with each other and that this unique journal must perish.

Address for correspondence: Centre for Psychoanalytic Studies, Eliot College, The University, Canterbury, Kent CT2 7NS, UK

The self-destructive subject: critical theory and the analysis of the unconscious and society

Anthony Elliott

Of all the attempts in modern social theory to transcend the split between the individual and society, it is in the work of the first generation of critical theory, the so-called Frankfurt School of the *Institut für Sozialforschung*, that the intersection of the social and psychic spheres is most explicitly proposed as an object of enquiry. Extending the insights of Weber and Lukàcs on the rationalization of modern consciousness, critical theory sought to integrate the study of the individual psyche within the analysis of cultural forms – an area long neglected by traditional Marxism. To do this, Freudian theory was used to bridge the abyss between the sociological and psychological realms in order to interpret aspects of the social whole.[1] In tracing out the boundaries and contours of the social and psychic worlds, the outstanding work of Herbert Marcuse and Theodor Adorno, the two most prominent critical theorists, has had a major impact on the concerns of contemporary social and political theory. Already dissatisfied with the work in this area of their former colleague Erich Fromm, Marcuse and

Free Associations (1993) Volume 3, Part 4 (No. 28): 503–44

Adorno sought from the early 1940s to map systematically the points of connection between culture, society and the human psyche. That the psychic and social domains had become divided was suggestively underscored by Adorno who argued that any such link offered by psychoanalysis could only be projected theoretically: 'The separation of sociology and psychology is both correct and false. False because it encourages the specialists to relinquish the attempt to know the totality which even the separation of the two demands; and correct in so far as it registers more intransigently the split that has actually taken place in reality than does the premature unification at the level of theory' (Adorno, 1967, p. 78).

In this paper I shall discuss several perspectives developed in the writings of Marcuse and Adorno on the theme of the unconscious and social relations. By focusing on their contributions to this specific theme, I shall necessarily have to sketch in rather broad strokes many aspects of their sociological and philosophical analyses. Moreover, in what follows I make no claim to deal with the astonishing range of critical studies published by these authors in areas such as aesthetics, music and philosophy. Rather, I shall analyse a number of central themes which are common to their rethinking of social and psychic boundaries. Of course, it must be stressed that the work of Marcuse and Adorno cannot be understood in any real sense as a unified enterprise. Even though they acknowledge a mutual indebtedness in their studies on the psyche and society, Marcuse and Adorno never worked directly together and were generally concerned with rather different linkages between these phenomena. But despite this, it is well established that there is something like a consensus in their theoretical orientations on the thesis of psychic fragmentation in the 'totally administered world'.[2] Accordingly, I shall try to tease out certain threads of consensus in their writings on the psyche and modern identity.

I shall begin by outlining the main parameters of the thesis of psychic fragmentation and their theories about the intersections of the psychic and social domains. The second section will present a critical assessment of Marcuse's and Adorno's reliance on Freud's early theory of the drives. There I shall try to show that, while identifying several key aspects of the intersections in psychic and social reality, their rather traditional and mechanical reading of Freud has not worn well and is, ultimately, deficient for the theorization of human subjectivity. What has been of lasting importance in Marcuse's and Adorno's appropriation of psychoanalysis, however, is their incisive analysis of the fragmentation of the human subject in modernity. In probing the limitations of a monadic view of psychic internalization in the third section, upon which their analysis of fragmentation is founded, I shall argue that the critique of domination developed by Marcuse and Adorno, while powerful, is based on a rather simplified and schematic interpretation of certain tendencies in modernity. The paper concludes by suggesting that these insights concerning the tendencies towards psychic fragmentation are, nevertheless, of considerable importance for the analysis of self-identity.

MARCUSE AND ADORNO ON SUBJECTIVITY AND THE UNCONSCIOUS

A characteristic feature of Marcuse's and Adorno's analyses of contemporary society and self-identity is their employment of the early 'biological' Freud – what I shall call *drive theory*. Rooted in the traditional Freudian vocabulary of an energetics of the mind, drive theory supposes that consciousness only gradually emerges from a differentiation from the unconscious as a result of the intrusion of external reality. As Marcuse puts it: 'the ego retains its birthmark as an "outgrowth" of the id. In relation to the id, the processes of the ego remain secondary processes' (1956, p. 31). In the antagonism ensuing in the shift from the pleasure principle to the reality principle, Marcuse and Adorno construct the ego, the centrepoint of consciousness, as the opponent of the drives. At first sight, this deployment of an instinctual conception of the psyche might be viewed as both a startling and problematic conceptual move. This is especially so if seen against the backdrop of the linguistic turn in much recent social theory and Anglo-American philosophy. But while Marcuse's and Adorno's use of drive theory is the main source of the theoretical limits and difficulties of much of their work, it also accounts for the scope and richness of their social critique. In penetrating the internal landscape of political and social domination within the individual, drive theory provided an effective framework for the first generation of critical theorists to map the depth-psychical consequences of social oppression in a manner unique to Marxism. It was for this reason that Marcuse and Adorno viewed the analytic revisions developed by the neo-Freudians, such as Hartmann, Horney and Sullivan, as a liberal attempt to rob psychoanalysis of its revolutionary potential. For the accounts of 'autonomous ego functions' provided by these ego-psychologists were said merely to perpetuate at a conceptual level the exaggerated illusions of autonomy and selfhood that mirrored the experiential nature of modernity.[3]

In connecting the central theoretical tenets of drive theory to an analysis of modern culture, a number of common preoccupations emerge in Marcuse's and Adorno's work. Among the most prominent are: the imbrication of historical and social factors in the structuring of the psyche; the subterranean points of connection between unconscious elements of self-identity and structures of domination; and the oppressive weight of technological reason upon modern social life. In what follows, I shall explore these themes in some detail. It is important initially to emphasize, however, that Marcuse's and Adorno's perspectives on these issues are substantially informed by the critique of consciousness developed in *Dialectic of Enlightenment*, written during the 1940s by Adorno and his Frankfurt colleague, Max Horkheimer. There are several psychoanalytic and sociological dimensions of this thesis, which is a speculative philosophy of history, that underpin Marcuse's and Adorno's writings on contemporary society and self-identity. The fundamental theme of *Dialectic of Enlightenment* is that the humanization of the drives, resulting in the transformation from natural instinct to the conscious self, produces a form of control of the ego. But this level of conscious control is double-edged, since it is established at the cost of a new inner division and sense of isolation and powerlessness. The Janus face of this process reveals itself in the repression of inner nature as the price of learning to dominate external nature. Subjectivity and rationality are constituted by the drive for self-preservation, but the separation from nature this involves also places, indeed fixes, the subject as victim. This is expressed in *Dialectic of Enlightenment* as follows: 'Man's domination over himself, which grounds his selfhood, is almost always the destruction of the subject in whose service it is undertaken; for the substance which is dominated, suppressed and dissolved through self-preservation is none other than that very life as a function of which the achievements of self-preservation are defined; it is, in fact, what is to be preserved' (Horkheimer and Adorno, 1973, p. 54).

MARCUSE'S MAPPING OF THE SOCIAL AND PSYCHIC FIELDS

In Marcuse's work during the 1950s there is a sustained attempt to reconceptualize this *dissolution* of the individual subject within the psychic and social fields of modernity. In his seminal work *Eros and Civilization*, Marcuse effects a systematic reconstruction of Freudian psychoanalysis into a progressive social-theoretical framework. Not surprisingly for someone who is both a Hegelian and dialectical Marxist, he argues that Freud's theory of the human subject must be rethought in the light of contemporary social developments. According to Marcuse, the insidious rise of systems of technology and bureaucracy has led to a breakdown of the stable features of self-identity. This breakdown has generated the progressive subsumption and manipulation of human subjects under modern technologies of the 'administered society'. As a consequence, Marcuse contends, the traditional object of psychoanalysis – the individual dissected into id, ego and super-ego – has become obsolescent in modern times. The 'bourgeois individual' has vanished. Throughout his career, however, Marcuse maintained that the principle of subjectivity cannot simply be discarded – as is the case in certain versions of post-structuralism. Instead, Marcuse tackles head-on the Freudian theory of instinctual drives, which have usually been viewed as implying the idea of a human nature and thus as inherently reactionary. The emphasis on an instinctual realm of the psyche, he argues, is in fact unequivocally positive. For whatever formations of repression come to predominate in society, the existence of the instinctual realm indicates that an alternative, personal core of selfhood always remains, timelessly residing in the unconscious. Hidden in psychoanalysis, Marcuse claims, there lies a true principle of identity.

In the opening chapters of *Eros and Civilization*, Marcuse traces the emergence of modern forms of self-identity through an analysis of some of Freud's most controversial claims. These include the oppositions between the pleasure principle and the reality principle, between the life and death instincts, and the view that civilization necessarily entails a repressive 'transformation of the libidinal drives. A distinctive facet of Marcuse's analysis of these ideas is his retracing of them within a comprehensive sociological and historical perspective. The aim of this reconceptualization, he writes, is to develop a social theory capable of mapping 'the mechanisms of social and political control in the depth dimension of instinctual drives and satisfactions'. To do this, he takes as fundamental to his analysis Freud's view that the human psyche is formed through contradiction; fractured through the painful split between the pleasure principle and the reality principle. In Freud's early work the psyche is regulated by two principles of functioning which are fundamentally antagonistic: the pleasure principle (connected with processes of unconscious satisfaction) and the reality principle (connected with the impinging of the object world on psychic reality). Marcuse speaks of these principles as the foundations of both subjecthood and culture: 'The vicissitudes of the instincts are the vicissitudes of the mental apparatus of civilization. The animal drives become human instincts under the influence of external reality' (1956, pp. 11–12). Through these intersecting processes, then, the individual comes to be 'socialized'; formed as 'a conscious thinking *subject*, geared to a rationality which is imposed upon him from outside' (1956, p. 16). In Freud's account, this surrender of the pleasure principle to the reality principle occurs in order to achieve a more durable and lasting kind of unconscious gratification. Marcuse, however, differs from Freud on this point. Taking the interplay of these principles to an extreme limit, Marcuse argues that contemporary social developments suggest there has been a 'transubstantiation' in the very notion of pleasure itself. Increasingly subjected to the crushing repressiveness of the current social order, unconscious gratification, as we will shortly examine, is conceived rather as a by-product of the pathologies of social power and domination.

Marcuse presses this Freudian theory of the repressive transformation of libidinal drives into an historical account of the ever-intensifying social coercion and domination of self-identity. The 'struggle with nature' is posited as the basis of human material existence; the renunciation of unconscious desire is taken to be necessary for social and cultural development. The level of repression for the progress of civilization, however, is not fixed. The increasing complexity of social organization demands that psychological repression be continually reinforced *and* increased. For Marcuse, this is 'the history of repression'. The transmutation of 'animal drives' into the constituted human 'subject' represents a shift from primitive societies to modern culture:

From	*To*
Immediate satisfaction	Delayed satisfaction
Pleasure	Restraint of pleasure
Play	Work
Receptiveness	Productiveness
Absence of repression	Security

Marcuse thus accepts the essentials of Freud's claim that the repression of unconscious drives has underpinned the existence of all historical forms of social organization (p. 12). But he differs from Freud in rejecting the view that psychological repression is necessarily the fate of humankind *in toto*. Marcuse's fundamental move is to introduce the argument that Freud generalizes the structure of psychological repression from a specific form of the reality principle, the economic order of capitalism, and extends it to all types of social organization. The crucial problem, as he formulates it, is that Freud's perspective is reductive: it too easily strips social dimensions of their force in the formation of the psyche. In contrast to Freud's fixed and ahistorical account, Marcuse's contention is that the content of the reality principle is the product of several determinations – it is structured through ideological, political and economic axes. Yet to capture these determinations,

Marcuse argues, it is not necessary to add a sociological account to Freudian theory since this reductive analysis already contains 'the elements of its opposite'. For Marcuse, Freud's theory of repression must instead be 'unfolded' and 'recaptured' through its own content.

While a certain amount of basic repression is necessary for the continuation of civilization, Marcuse postulates that processes of repression are always structured within the particular constitution of the social world. Though the 'reality principle demands a considerable degree and scope of repressive control over the instincts', he argues, 'the specific historical institutions of the reality principle and the specific interests of domination introduce additional controls over and above those indispensable for civilized human association' (p. 37). In order more adequately to separate the specific forms of socio-historical domination from their biological underpinnings, Marcuse introduces two crucial neologisms: surplus-repression and the performance principle (pp. 35ff.). Surplus-repression refers to those specific forms of political and ideological domination that induce extra-libidinal renunciations. It comprises any restrictions placed upon the libidinal drives which regroove basic repressions in the interests of domination. The performance principle refers to the specific cultural form of 'reality' which is constituted by the economic order of capitalism. According to Marcuse, the central features of this domination include: the restrictions placed on sexuality by the monogamic-patriarchal nuclear family; the hierarchical division of labour experienced in late-capitalist society; and the pathologies of mass commodified culture. It operates through the stratification of human subjects into competitive economic 'roles' and 'performances'. As a modality that engenders repression which is predominantly surplus, it is internally connected to the reproduction and maintenance of asymmetrical social relations of power. For Marcuse, it is this entwinement of surplus-repression and the performance principle which has led to the progressive loss of individual autonomy in modern society.

It will be clear by now that the main purpose of Marcuse's work is to reformulate the Freudian theory of repression in order more adequately to comprehend certain contemporary intersections between the psychic and social fields. Marcuse was not content, though, to analyse the points of connection between the social and psychic realms at such a high level of abstraction. Throughout a series of publications, he sought to connect his account of the increasing repressiveness of modern social processes with an analysis of specific cultural and political changes affecting the processes of identity formation. In Marcuse's view, Freudian psychoanalysis is yet again valuable to social theory, when historically contextualized, since it explores in detail the processes of identity formation during the liberal phase of capitalism. Crucial to this understanding of the constitution of the 'bourgeois individual', he argues, is the Oedipus complex. Through the dialectic of resistance and compliance to a feared outside authority figure (the father), the individual subject in the liberal epoch slowly forged a unity of the self and won a sense of human autonomy. It was through the processes of internalization and identification with the father that the subject came to reproduce the bourgeois relationship to authority. Measured in terms of the dialectic of Enlightenment, however, this primary identification with authority is viewed by Marcuse as both enabling and repressive. It generates a degree of autonomy through constituting selfhood and yet perpetuates domination since it is based upon a prior acceptance of authority. But while autonomy may only be partial during the epoch of liberal capitalism, such a social order does provide the *possibilities* for authentic subjecthood and new social experience.

On Marcuse's account, however, today's social conditions are significantly different from those in which Freud analysed the formation of self-identity. The massive social and industrial transformations which have occurred this century, and changes in systems of economy and technology as well as cultural production, have all resulted in a radical escalation in psychological repression. For Marcuse, the more the new technological society has advanced, the more repression has become surplus. In order to sustain the asymmetrical relations of power characteristic of the current social order, the immense productive capacities released from technology, modernism and monopoly capital have been turned back upon the subject with a vengeance. Repression is at once made self-regulative *and* self-intensifying. These developments are directly linked by Marcuse to changes in the role of the father in the context of individual development. The transition from market to monopoly capitalism, Marcuse argues, signals a major change in the function of the family in the reproduction of social and economic relationships. The position of the father, in particular, is thought to be rendered vunerable through a wide variety of sources: his declining economic status, subject to inflation and unemployment, means his image of power and strength as an 'authority figure' is shattered. As a consequence, individuals are said to forge identifications less and less through Oedipal processes. Instead, they turn increasingly to a range of extra-familial author-ities. This ties in directly with the intrusion into family rela-tionships of a host of external forces of socialization. These include: the mass media industries, the modern state, the pressures of commodified culture and so on. For Marcuse, the modern subject tends to identify increasingly with the mechanical and rigid value-systems which these agencies promote. This is said to result in a disintegration of ego autonomy. Hence, the individual's psycholo-gical state is marked more and more by conventional and stereotyped modes of thinking and affect.

Only a few further elements in Marcuse's treatment of the structuring properties of modern self-identity deserve mention here. In a highly subtle treatment of the organization of social life under capitalism, Marcuse argues that the erotogenic zones of the body undergo a profound psychic restructuring for the mainte-nance and reproduction of alienated labour. He contends that this can be discerned in the shift from sexuality as 'polymorphous-perverse' – without any temporal and spatial constraints on its expression – to the hierarchical and centralized organization of the libidinal drives in modern work relations. 'Originally the organism in its totality and in all its activities and relationships is a potential field for sexuality, dominated by the pleasure principle. And precisely for this reason it must be desexualized in order to carry out unpleasurable work, in order, in fact, to live in a context of unpleasurable work' (1970, pp. 8–9). This 'desexualization' is achieved through the channelling of libido into 'repressive desub-limation': the harnessing of erotic energy to the performance principle. This occurs through the repressive distribution of time in modern societies. The structuring of the average working day, the routinization and regimentation of daily life, and so on, all contri-bute to the subjection of libidinal relationships to the interests of domination. But equally important are the spatial repressions placed on the libidinal drives. Not only is non-procreative sex restricted so as to release libidinal energy for alienated labour, but there is also a repressive centralization of the libido which mirrors the dominative rationality of liberal morality. In sum, there is a centralization of the various aims of the libidinal drives into one desired object (usually of the other sex), resulting in the dominance of genitality over all other libidinal forms of expression. Thus, Marcuse argues, modern sexuality only exists 'part-time' (1956, p. 47). Through this repression of the erotogenic zones of the libidinal drives, the body becomes 'free' for use as labour power. Such a restructuring of the psyche is held to cement the very dis-simulation of administered domination, providing the foundation for a high degree of integration in modern industrial societies.

ADORNO ON SELF-IDENTITY AND NARCISSISM

In a series of essays written in the 1940s and '50s, Adorno also examines the points of connection between self-identity and human autonomy.[4] Defending the importance of Freud's work, Adorno argues that psychoanalysis explores in detail the classic processes of identity-formation in the late-nineteenth and early-twentieth cen-turies. In contrast to Marcuse, he is not much concerned with the methodological linkages of the psychic and social fields. On philosophical grounds, Adorno refused to articulate the conceptual foundations of such concepts. Rather, he employs psychoanalytic theory to understand recent changes in the psychic dynamics of modern social processes. As Martin Jay observes, 'what instead drew Adorno to the early Freud was the way in which his theory unflinchingly registered the traumas of contemporary existence. Telling the harsh truth was itself a kind of resistance to the acceptance of those traumas as inevitable' (1984, p. 90). A central purpose of Adorno's appropriation of psychoanalytic theory is to juxtapose the stasis of nature with the dynamism of the social-historical world. Psychic processes must be rethought in the light of modern social conditions better to conceptualize the increasingly compulsive features of self-identity in the 'administered world'. For Adorno, the internal contours of self-identity demanded such deciphering since the compulsive drive for self-preservation has become all but invisible in modernity. He expresses this perpetuation of the subject's 'compulsive identity' in *Negative Dialectics* as follows: 'Since self-preservation has been precarious and difficult for eons, the power of its instrument, the ego drives, remains all but irresistible even after technology has virtually made self-preservation easy; that power surpasses the one of the object drives whose specialist, Freud, misconceived it' (1973, p. 349).

According to Adorno, the nature of Freud's misconception concerns the ego. This is so, Adorno feels, because the ego is the representative of contradictory functions in Freud's metapsychology. As he puts it, 'the ego is supposed to be both, *qua* consciousness, the opposite of repression, and, *qua* unconscious, the repressive agency itself' (1967, p. 86). As the representative of both cognitive operations and the co-ordinator of libidinal impulses, then, there is an immanent contradiction at the centre of ego functions. In order to live and operate in society, the ego functions through cognitive testing and yet, because of the repressive and pathological dimensions of modern social processes, it must also effect unconscious prohibitions. Throughout the liberal phase of capitalism, these contradictions are forged through a resistance to, and internalization of, the authority of the father in the Oedipus complex. With the ushering in of the 'administered world of late capitalism', however, Adorno concurs with Marcuse that there has been an eclipse of the social conditions from which individuation develops. Internalization fails. As a consequence, what ego autonomy there was from the bourgeois humanist legacy is today increasingly undermined. The possibility for human subjects to experience caring emotional relationships and authentic sociality is shattered through the increasing weakness of the ego. 'Where the ego fails to develop its intrinsic potential for self-differentiation', Adorno writes, 'it will regress, especially toward what Freud called ego-libido, to which it is most closely related, or will at least mingle its conscious functions with unconscious ones. What actually wanted to get beyond the unconscious then re-enters the service of the unconscious and may thus even strengthen its force' (1967, p. 87). Less and less an agency of critical self-reflection, the subject's own ego is taken as the central love-object for modern selfhood.

In Adorno's view, these developments influence the shape of subjectivity in two central ways: there is a chronic weakness of ego-identity and, subsequently, a dramatic rise in narcissism. The narcissistically weakened self, he affirms, becomes an increasingly prevalent character type in modern society since the requirements of late capitalism demand a reversal in self-awareness. In Adorno's view, the historical precursor to these developments can be seen in the rise of fascist mass movements this century. In 'Freudian theory and the pattern of fascist propaganda', written in 1951, Adorno argues that Freud's work on group psychology foresaw the rise of fascist movements without sliding into the regressive crowd psychology of Le Bon and others (1951, pp. 118–37). The psychological mechanisms uncovered by Freud's analyses of group processes are vitally significant, Adorno argues, since they draw attention to the ways in which individuals yield to the political manipulation of external, social agencies. Following Freud, Adorno affirms that when in a large group the individual tends to identify less with its own 'ego-ideals' and more with impersonal 'group ideals'. This is said to discourage individual autonomy through the undoing of unconscious repressions – thereby releasing the powerful destructive energies necessary for the underpinning of any fascist collectivity. The key mechanism for this release of violent and sadistic unconscious drives is identification. For it is through an identification with the fascist leader that the follower is unconsciously able to introject the desensitized and ruthless celebrations of brute power itself. This process of identification, which contains a strong narcissistic dimension, is capable of making 'the beloved object part of oneself'. According to Adorno, such narcissistic tendencies are becoming a crucial part of our most paranoid identifications in modern social processes as a whole. As he explains it:

> this process has a psychological dimension, but it also indicates a growing tendency toward the abolition of psychological motivation in the old, liberalistic sense. Such motivation is systematically controlled and absorbed by social mechanisms which are directed from above . . . The psychological 'impoverishment' of the subject that 'surrendered itself to the object' . . . anticipates almost with clairvoyance the postpsychological de-individualized social atoms which form the fascist collectivities. (1951, p. 136)

According to this view, the present-day weakness of the ego renders the unconscious liable to the formations of domination and social power itself. The libidinal drives, which were traditionally co-ordinated by the autonomy of the ego, become increasingly absorbed by destructive and alienating social forces – such as fascism and the culture industry. Thus, there is a breakdown of the vital distinctions between consciousness and the unconscious.

The interplay of these main concepts – narcissism, identification, and their interconnections in social processes – is further elaborated in Adorno's essay 'Sociology and psychology'.[5] Due to the increasingly instrumental and reified forms of modern social processes, according to Adorno, the ego must forgo self-awareness in the interests of self-preservation. By withdrawing into the unconscious, the ego is said to be increasingly rigidified through narcissistic illusions of self-containment. This taxing, and ultimate demise, of the ego is expressed by Adorno as follows:

> The social power-structure hardly needs the mediating agencies of ego and individuality any longer . . . The truly contemporary types are those whose actions are motivated neither by an ego nor, strictly speaking, unconsciously, but mirror objective trends like an automaton. Together they enact a senseless ritual to the beat of a compulsively repetitive rhythm and become emotionally impoverished: with the destruction of the ego, narcissism, or its collective derivatives, is heightened. (1967, p. 95)

In Adorno's view, then, narcissism comes to replace internalization. Fathers, as representatives of bourgeois authority, are no longer dominating figures worthy of identification and emulation. As David Held comments, for Adorno the individual subject in modern times no longer wants 'to become like his father but, rather, like the image projected by the culture industry (or by fascist demagogues, as in Nazi Germany)' (1980, p. 133). The decline of the ego thus leads to a profound modification of the nature of unconscious drives. In short, the unconscious becomes exposed towards what were characteristic ego goals (Adorno, 1967, pp. 87–8).

Adorno thus concludes this investigation into modern self-identity by advancing the provocative thesis that social mediations become fully pressed into the service of the unconscious. According to this standpoint, psychic reality unfolds through the direct manipulation of unconscious drives and impulses by social agencies. Libidinal relationships are today mobilized, structured and sustained through the organized domination of the culture industry. Unconscious gratification, increasingly centred around destructive impulses, is directly manipulated through phenomena of repetitive cultural production. Purposeless diversions and the encouragement of empty pursuits are valorized by the communications media – through the dissemination of advertising, films, pop music and so on. As Adorno puts this, a 'brutal standardizing society arrests all differentiation, and to this end it exploits the primitive core of the unconscious. Both conspire to annihilate the mediating ego; the triumphant archaic impulses, the victory of id over ego, harmonize with the triumph of society over the individual' (1967, p. 95). Passively handed to the fully rationalized world, powerless to respond in anything but the most paralyzed manner to every social stimulus and demand, the psychic structure of the individual subject regresses to the planned obsolescence on which the social structure is predicated. The adaptation of the unconscious, Adorno affirms, becomes an invisible 'inner continuation' of a society fully structured through instrumental and technological reason.

At this stage, it might be useful to try to bring together the main threads of the arguments considered so far. We can distinguish four central aspects (no doubt more could be found) of Marcuse's and Adorno's interpretation of modern processes of repression and fragmentation. They may be regarded as follows:

1 *A theory of selfhood based upon internalization*: In the liberal epoch of market capitalism, self-identity is understood as being forged through the internalization of paternal authority. Connecting Freud's account of the Oedipus complex to the themes of the dialectic of Enlightenment, however, Marcuse and Adorno argue that this process of identity-formation is double-edged. The dialectic of resistance and submission to paternal authority in the process of individuation both constitutes and painfully splits the human subject. The forging of self-identity is thus internally tied to the social-historical process of internalizing authority.

2 *The eclipse of internalization*: With the ushering in of the 'administered world of late capitalism', Marcuse and Adorno contend that the social and political role of the family in identity-formation is defused and undermined. The process of individuation, through internalization, is 'eclipsed'. Replacing the relative degree of individual autonomy once generated through the internalization of paternal authority, the rationalized world of commodified culture and depersonalized social relations generates a failure in ego development. As Marcuse argues, the modern subject's 'ego has shrunk to such a degree that the multiform antagonistic processes between id, ego and superego cannot unfold themselves in their classic form' (1956, p. 99).

3 *The manipulation of the unconscious*: According to Marcuse and Adorno, the movement from the liberal phase of capitalism to the 'totally administered society' eliminates the requirements for an ego that is relatively adaptive and has a measure of autonomy. The result of this is the

emergence of new social forms of repression. Discovering a hidden form of the drive for self-preservation, the ego is said to have withdrawn into the unconscious. As such, the relations between consciousness and the unconscious are fully betrayed by logical incoherence and fragmentation. It is true that a display of individuality and spontaneity is retained; as is witnessed in the so-called 'liberation' of sexuality in modern times. But even this 'private space', Marcuse remarks, is just another commodity sphere in which the images and products of sexuality can be disseminated, thereby heightening the curse of 'repressive desublimation' (1966, pp. 74–7). Thus, the manipulation of unconscious processes by the 'totally administered society' produces what Adorno evocatively terms the 'boundlessly elastic, subjectless subject' (1967, p. 85).

4 *The repression of consciousness*: In the liberal epoch, when internalization reigned supreme, the formation of the self revealed its Janus face in the repression of libidinal drives as the price of self-control. What is said to distinguish modernity from previous forms of social existence, however, is that it is now the ego that comes into a state of conflict and is, ultimately, rendered obsolete. This fourth point is already implied by the other three. The increasing isolation of the modern subject in situations of powerlessness serves to constrain feeling and action, thereby subverting awareness and perception. Consciousness and the capacity for critical self-reflection become repressed. Drawing on the work of Franz Alexander, Marcuse speaks of an 'automization' and 'corporealization' of the psyche and rational cognition. As he explains this, the 'defence consists chiefly in a strengthening of controls not so much over the instincts as over consciousness, which, if left free, might recognize the work of repression in the bigger and better satisfaction of needs' (1956, p. 94). Accordingly, subjecthood is granted a certain degree of autonomy for the purpose of self-preservation, but not enough to threaten the content and form of the social structure. With

the repression of cognition, as well as human desire, the modern subject enters an historical context of unprecedented fragmentation.

REPRESSION, DOMINATION AND THE SOCIAL ORDER

The work of Marcuse and Adorno offers one of the most challenging descriptions of the interrelations between subjectivity and the unconscious, on the one hand, and the effects of social and political organization, on the other, wrought by recent historical developments. Throughout their analyses, the nature of the unconscious is intimately related to social and historical features of modern life. The matrix of problems arising from modernity, as it is posed here, hinges on the observed connections between increasingly evident social changes – economic and political but also changes of media in cultural production – and the overwhelming repression of the modern subject. As we have seen, Marcuse and Adorno locate the origins of the fragmentation of the subject in the drive to self-preservation. In the liberal phase of the economic order of capitalism, the forging of self-identity reveals its Janus face in the repression of unconscious drives as the price of self-control and a measure of autonomy. In repressing its own libidinal drives in the name of autonomy, the drive to self-preservation inflicts a permanent damage on the self. This damage *is* the formation of selfhood brutally shot through with inner division, isolation and repetitive compulsion. This ambivalently emancipatory and repressive forging of the ego for Marcuse and Adorno, as we have charted, is most clearly discernible in the dialectic of struggle and submission in the Oedipus complex. Introjecting the dominative reason of the father in order to win a sense of selfhood, the emergence of autonomy is understood as internally tied to the prior submission to a repressive authority. The shift into the 'administered world' of late capitalism, however, signals the complete breakdown of this already fragile sense of self-identity. According to Marcuse and Adorno, the previous antagonisms between the pleasure principle and the reality principle, the individual and society, are all but obliterated. Instead, a new and more powerful form of ideological incorporation arises.

The individual subject today is incorporated within the dominant cultural values of society by the manipulation of unconscious processes.

At the outset, it is important to stress that this conceptual structure provides a critical perspective on self-identity and modern social processes. Marcuse's and Adorno's work offer particularly sophisticated accounts of the interrelations between consciousness and the unconscious. In this view, the simultaneously emancipatory and repressive forging of consciousness is internally connected to a similar structure of antagonism in the unconscious. This fundamentally ambivalent conscious/unconscious dualism is, paradoxically, the social foundation of both creativity and oppression, empathy and violence, autonomy and heteronomy. The general features of this view of the internal complexity of self-identity are of signal importance when contrasted with much present-day social and cultural theory, which either rejects or is silent about such crucial concepts as identity, subjectivity, the psyche and so on. For even when Marcuse and Adorno announce the 'obsolescence of the subject', their analyses still hold firm to the subjective principle. As Peter Dews notes of this standpoint:

> the forging of the ego, as the form of organization of the drives, contains a moment of freedom, in so far as it is only through this process that human beings acquire the ability to foresee, calculate and withhold which frees them from the contingencies of inner and outer nature . . . At the same time, however, the dialectic of Enlightenment consists in the fact that ever-intensifying self-restraint leads to the abolition of that very spontaneity of the self which calculating rationality was intended to preserve. (1987, p. 141)

Thus, as Dews comments, no matter how apparently repressive or incorporative social manipulation has become, it is this 'moment of freedom' from which Marcuse and Adorno project the *principle of identity* as the basis for social change. Similarly, their stress on this principle of self-identity as comprising both consciousness and the unconscious makes plain the central limitations of current postmodernist debates on the psyche. For, in their more naturalistic versions, such accounts have tended to hypothesize a split between a repressive order of consciousness and the emancipatory disorder of the libidinal drives. The result of this view, as represented in Gilles Deleuze's and Felix Guattari's theory of 'desiring machines' (1977), is a naive espousal of human liberation through the free play of libidinal drives. For Marcuse and Adorno, however, such a one-sided privileging of the unconscious is merely symptomatic of the very crisis of modernity – epitomized in the fragmentation of the subject. Reconciliation is to be found neither in the destruction of consciousness (in which there would be no subject left to enjoy any newly founded sensibility) nor by a reversion to a more 'natural' harmony, but by the transformation of society itself.

Yet it is also worth noting that Marcuse's and Adorno's project is ambivalent in political terms. On the one hand, it is a radical critique of the subterranean connections between the rise of modern institutions and the repression of the individual subject. The increasing normalization and alienation of modern social processes is shown to be deeply interfused with the subjection of the individual to mechanical passivity and conformity. Repression of the self is the converse side of a destructive and pathological social order which forces human subjects into an empty, narcissistic concern with the ego. On the other hand, the view that the drive to self-preservation is marked by a compulsion that hardens into an ever-intensifying repression of the self leads to a dangerous neglect of the complexities of social modernization. Marcuse's and Adorno's notion of identity is so focused on compulsive unconscious drives that it fails adequately to take into account the different modalities of political and ideological forces which impinge upon everyday life. Not all systems of economy and bureaucracy are equally repressive of self-identity. Yet it is doubtful that their account of self-identity has the conceptual means of separating the features of the social system which can provide a gain in autonomous expression from those which reproduce repression and domination. It is in this context that some commentators have argued that Marcuse and Adorno tend to ignore the vital political differences between the principles of liberal democracy and fascism.

These political ambivalences, it seems to me, have their basis in deeper conceptual problems. What is perhaps most difficult to accept in Marcuse's and Adorno's analyses is their specific use of the notion of repression to explicate the general contours of social development. If repression is the result of the drive to self-preservation *in toto*, as Marcuse and Adorno claim, then self-identity can only be viewed as inherently compulsive and destructive. Yet there are reasons for believing that this view simplifies the highly complex psychic processes involved in the repression of the libidinal drives. Psychic life, as Freud shows, often has a compulsive aspect to it. But to claim that this is unequivocally the main dynamic of modern self-identity seems to me a highly dubious argument. If Marcuse's and Adorno's standpoint is wrong, as I believe it to be, it is necessary to retrace the processes by which repression becomes deeply locked into culture and societal reproduction. My argument, broadly speaking, is that repression is constituted, not through a monadic drive to self-preservation, but through a complex and intricate process in which unconscious drives intersect in our relations with others.

In offering some critical reflections on the work of Marcuse and Adorno, my aim is to tease out certain tensions and difficulties in their conceptualization of the links between the psychic and social realms. In the following paragraphs I cannot attempt to elaborate my arguments in the full detail that they require. Instead, I shall, for the sake of clarity, focus my critical comments by briefly listing three problems or aporias in Marcuse's and Adorno's arguments: theses which are particularly questionable and problematic. They are first, that repression is constituted by the drive to self-preservation; second, that the process of repression involves a 'subjugation' of the libidinal drives, of 'inner nature'; and third, that the increasing complexity of societal modernization necessarily demands increased psychological repression. In criticizing these viewpoints, I shall suggest that it is necessary to break with such presuppositions in a radical way.

The first aporia, then, is Marcuse's and Adorno's compression of the complex and intricate processes of repression into the single mechanism of the 'drive for self-preservation'. This view, as we have charted, appears in various formulations. But essentially, it involves the following claim. The drive to self-preservation arises, and is necessary, to release the self from its bondage to nature. This drive shifts the individual subject from the pleasure principle, an order of gratification and fulfilment, into the repressive confines of the reality principle, a culturally specific order of domination and exploitation. Moreover, once established, the drive to self-preservation becomes both self-regulative and increasingly opaque to everyday consciousness. Derived from Freud's early model of the psyche, the self-preservative instincts are theoretically brought in to account for the 'transmutation' from 'animal instincts' to the fully constituted 'human subject'. However, the use of the drive for self-preservation in this connection is a hazardous one. It has a peculiarly shadowy status in Freud's writings and, after the revisions necessitated by the introduction of the theory of narcissism, it was later subsumed within the general notion of the life drives. While Freud certainly referred to the bodily functions necessary for the preservation of the subject generically, he failed ever to trace out whether such functions are actually libidinal drives or biological necessities.

However, in later psychoanalytic doctrine there has been a broad consensus that the self-preservative functions are part of the biological structure of the body and not of the libidinal drives. (A summary of these trends is given in Laplanche and Pontalis, 1973, pp. 220–22.) On this view, the instincts for self-preservation – the biological requirements for warmth, nourishment, shelter and so on – do not play a determining role in the dynamics of repression. So, too, the interplay between the pleasure principle and the reality principle does not apply to this sector of the psyche. As Laplanche and Pontalis comment, it is important to stress

> the artificiality of attempts to establish a strict parallelism, genetically speaking, between the self-preservative functions and the sexual instincts, on the grounds that both are equally subject to begin with to the pleasure principle, before gradually coming under the dominion of the reality principle. In fact the self-preservative functions ought instead to be assigned to the

side of the reality principle from the start, and the sexual. instincts to the side of the pleasure principle. (1973, p. 221)

This viewpoint is drived from Jacques Lacan, who makes the analytical distinction between need, demand and desire in order to transcend the elision in Freud's writings of libidinal drives and biological needs. From this perspective, a clear terminological distinction emerges between libidinal drives, which because of their plasticity are treated as desires; and the functions of self-preservation, which due to their instinctual rigidity are treated as biological needs.[6] It is within the former domain, unconscious desire, that the dynamics of repression are structured.

These psychoanalytical interpretations suggest there are serious shortcomings in Marcuse's and Adorno's view that the phenomenon of repression, produced today at levels of crippling proportion, is the result of a 'drive to self-preservation'. Indeed, Marcuse's opening claim in *Eros and Civilization* that self-identity is at once forged *ánd* repressed when 'animal drives become human instincts under the influence of external reality' begins to look faintly absurd. For it seeks to compress the complex processes through which the libidinal drives and object world interfuse through the specification of a single sovereign mechanism. My comments, however, should not be taken to imply that the needs of self-preservation are entirely unconnected with the formation of repressed desire. The emergence of unconscious desire is originally inseparable from the satisfaction of biological needs. Yet, as Freud tirelessly repeats, the specific configurations of repressed desire only develop through being separated out from the satisfaction of these needs. Repressed desire emerges through, yet is radically *severed* from, the needs of self-preservation. As regards social development, such processes of unconscious pleasure and gratification are similarly separated out from the satisfaction of these transhistorical, fixed needs. Indeed, it is in this separating out of the unconscious, in and through which cultural production is structured, that the mysterious connections between repression and cultural domination, desire and law, are located. Against Marcuse and Adorno, it can be argued that repression is not organized into set practices of compulsion and repetition. Desire and repression, at once libidinal and aggressive, swerve onto many *different* paths of social and historical development. These may include the possibilities of friendship, love or the forging of communal identity. Alternatively, they may be drawn towards practices of exploitation characteristic of the contemporary capitalist order, the possibility of nuclear war or the obliteration of cultural minorities. But my point, for reasons I shall later try to identify, is that these paths of desire develop through our concrete implication with others. They do not operate, as Marcuse and Adorno suggest, through an already fully-fashioned compulsive drive to self-preservation.

This latter view, that repression is constituted through our concrete interaction with others, leads directly to the second aporia of Marcuse's and Adorno's work: their tendency to imagine that repression involves a 'subjugation' of pre-formed libidinal drives. Baldly stated, it is supposed that there is a 'subjugation' or 'transformation' of originally spontaneous libidinal drives into the repressive confines of self-control and calculation. Modern social processes, in short, are seen as placing obstructions upon the expression and attainment of libidinal gratification. Now it is undeniably the case that the forging of self-identity depends to some degree upon a repression and mastery of unconscious drives. But it is quite mistaken to conceptualize self-identity as arising from a monadic 'subjugation' of an original spontaneous desire. The view that there is a personal and timeless core of subjugated desire is inadequate, since its conception of repression is too simple. It is not the case that individuals have some fully-formed core of selfhood which is not already part of the everyday contexts that define their immersion in the social world. What is missing in this understanding of repression is any focus on the place of *human relationships*, of the connections between self and other.

Anthony Wilden has persuasively argued that the use in critical theory of an 'orthodox' Freudian model of the instincts actually *suppresses* its conceptual focus on the problems of alienated human relationships (1969, pp. 196–245). The central problem is that such a focus on the instinctual realm of the psyche leads to a neglect of the place of other persons in understanding phases of repression at both the individual and social levels. The difficulties of a monadic view of repression are described by Wilden in the following way:

> whatever the biological instincts (needs) require of the biological individual, the human drives (desire) are the new products of organization as such, and at another level. They are discontinuous with what went before or below; the drives are social by their very nature. They come to us, not from ourselves, but from our relation to the Other; they are not the simple continuous transformation or repression or subjugation of something else in us or in our past. (1969, pp. 221–2)

Characterized in this way, the libidinal drives are not something that is already formed and which, subsequently, undergoes the pressure of repression. As Freud's later writings make plain, repression is an outcome of specific processes of identification and interaction *between* human beings. Desire and repression are constituted at one stroke through a mutual process of human expression, structured within specific social contexts. This theme connects to wider issues about the nature of self-identity, which I will consider in greater detail in the next section.

Finally, the third aporia concerns Marcuse's and Adorno's conception that social and cultural development has been associated with intensified levels of psychological repression. For them, repression is a specifically historical notion which is the key to interpreting processes of societal modernization. The transition from traditional societies to modern culture has entailed the inculcation of increasingly repressive prohibitions. And this heightened degree of psychological repression is directly contrasted to the 'playfulness' and 'spontaneous expression' of emotion in less complex societies. Several commentators, however, have argued that Marcuse's and Adorno's appeal to the notion of a 'spontaneous self', which exists prior to the inception of social development, is nostalgic and regressive (see Jameson, 1988, pp. 109–10). This criticism is surely right. But it is necessary to question the contours of these claims further since their implications for this study are vitally significant. That there are major differences, in the quantity of libidinal repression, between traditional forms of social organization and modern culture is a highly dubious hypothesis. Sociological and anthropological research refutes the idea that there is any distinct correlation between psychological repression and the level of material and economic complexity in different societies.[7] On the contrary, as regards the repression of emotion and desire, the existence of firmly entrenched moral prohibitions and other renunciations can be said to have characterized the daily life of many early forms of social existence.

This should not be taken to imply, however, that the character of subjecthood and modern personal relations has not been significantly transformed with the major institutional transitions brought into existence by modernity. The accelerating changes in the social world this century have intimately interlocked with the nature of selfhood and the unconscious. But such transformations have equally accompanied attempts by subjects to create new forms of personal relations and authentic sociality. It is not the case, then, that human social development can be reduced to a linear dynamic of an intensified, tortured psychological repression.

It is necessary to resist the view that repression is a historically cumulative process. The 'separation' of a personal, social identity from psychic instances by the 'barrier of repression' is fundamental to all societies, notwithstanding the vast cross-cultural differences in forms of libidinal expression. The existence of the 'barrier of repression' within all types of social systems, however, does not mean that we cannot generalize about the repressiveness of given social arrangements. For this is surely what is so attractive to social theory about Marcuse's and Adorno's conceptual structure. But, characteristically, the standard that tends to be offered in their work for assessing cultural domination is an implicit focus on the *quantity* of repression – the amount of libidinal gratification which is denied the individual by society. The relation between societal modernization and repression is rarely explicitly considered in terms of the *quality* of human social relationships that a given social order makes possible. Yet this is clearly not because either Marcuse or Adorno were insensitive to the destructive and oppressive effects that modern social processes inscribe upon self-identity. On the contrary, their work represents an urgent plea against such subjective deformations. But in analysing processes of dominative rationality and social power through a monadic conception of the psyche, the subtlety of their cultural criticism is certainly limited by the crudity of their understanding of the nature of repression.

Of course, it might be argued that Marcuse's account of surplus-repression is precisely such an integration of these unconscious elements of selfhood within intersubjective, political and ideological dimensions of social life. But even the notion of a 'surplus' accumulation of denied gratification is still inadequate, since its account of the connections between repression and society is too simple. Marcuse is correct, I believe, in conceptualizing processes of repression within the asymmetrical relations of power of contemporary social processes. But the way in which these processes are traced out too drastically reduces the space – at once psychic and social – of individual subjects. To claim that basic libidinal renunciations are regrooved by 'surplus-repression' as a result of the configurations of monogamous sexuality and commodified culture – entities which are presented in his analyses as external, social forces – results in the paradoxical situation of a reductionist sociologism that Marcuse sought to escape from in the first place. The problem, as Jean Laplanche comments (1969, p. 133), is that Marcuse fails to specify in what manner basic repression might be said to be reconstituted as 'surplus-repression'. Marcuse's notion is certainly a model of socialized repression, but not one in which there is a connecting track between the conscious and unconscious formations of representation on the one side and the increasing control of these states of representation by actual social and institutional relations on the other. Against Marcuse, the relations of domination and exploitation that become deeply layered within unconscious elements of self-identity are not simply pressed in from the social and ideological field. The relation between social processes and repression has to be understood instead as a psychically creative process of production. While human subjects are 'positioned' within social, political and ideological relations, it must be acknowledged that such positions are necessarily also invested with psychic energy – which, in turn, 'feeds back' into the social world. It is only within this dual process that specific sites of cultural renewal and struggle become intelligible.

THE FORMATION OF SELF-IDENTITY

The deficiencies in Marcuse's and Adorno's account of repression are connected to a fundamental assumption about the nature of self-identity. This is the assumption that the constitution of self-identity occurs against the backdrop of a monadic and uniform introjection of the law of social and cultural relations. Repressive subjecthood is traced as the result of the internalization of the authority of the father. A reliance on this monadic theory of identity formation is perhaps directly responsible, I believe, for some of the main problems of Marcuse's and Adorno's view of subjectivity. It also connects, as I shall try to show in the next section, with problems in their account of contemporary culture. One major line of criticism on these issues, developed by post-modernist critics, has been to deconstruct the very goals of 'individuation' and 'autonomy' embedded in such a standpoint. From this perspective, a standard response is to seek to demonstrate that such metaphysical notions act in complicity with the dominant Western modes of understanding, thereby only reproducing modernist illusions that serve to structure the very crisis of modernity itself. In what follows, I want to take a different approach. Rather, I shall argue that the theory of internalization and repressive selfhood developed by Marcuse and Adorno is ultimately incoherent since it fails to comprehend the processes – at once psychic and social – in which self-identity is constituted. To do this, it is necessary to retrace certain assumptions which underpin Marcuse's and Adorno's account of internalization – the traces of which latter, in the present epoch, are said to contain the last vestiges of resistance to social domination.

A number of issues concerning the plausibility of Marcuse's and Adorno's account of the formation of self-identity can be raised. First, there is much to be made of the oft-repeated charge that their account of the process of internalization is unduly restrictive. It will be recalled that this account of internalization posits a one-shot emergence of individuation through the resolution and acceptance of the authority of the father in the Oedipus complex. Through an identification with paternal authority, the subject is said eventually to win a sense of autonomy and develop a social identity. In doing so, however, the ego itself becomes an intrapsychic agent of authority and domination. The internalization of parental authority is set up as an 'inner compulsion' of subjecthood. In Marcuse's and Adorno's view, then, a fateful impasse arises, since individuation leads to its own internal destruction. Accordingly, the specific aspects of self-identity where resistance might be thought to exist – in critical self-reflection, rationality and so on – are already internally tied to the acceptance of repressive authority. In turn, this thesis is used as a benchmark to assess the political structures of modern societies. The formation of self-identity and rationality is seen as being unavoidably tied to the repressive forces of political domination and oppression through which the social order is reproduced and sustained.

There are many problems, however, with the general theoretical assumptions which inform this account of the process of internalization. Approaches such as Marcuse's and Adorno's, with their assumption that self-identity is an internalized continuation of repressive authority, fail to explore what is most in need of explanation: the active psychic processes enmeshed in the construction of subjectivity and selfhood. Freud's writings demonstrate that there is a rich diversity of ways in which human subjects (always uniquely) pass through the Oedipus complex. The labyrinth of emotional identifications forged within this phase of development cannot be reduced to a single mechanism by which social authority is inculcated. An individual subject's relations with others and external authorities are highly complex matters, involving factors such as the *psychic construction* of early object-loss, the emotional context of the social surround and so on. Yet, Marcuse and Adorno fail to accord these variations any substantive consideration. Consequently, their account of the links between the Oedipus complex and the psychic movements towards autonomy are one-sided. Their interpretation of the Oedipus complex, paradoxically, tends to mirror the more rigid and pathological aspects of the very social processes that they are concerned to probe and criticize. It is an interpretation which privileges rationality over emotion, law over creativity. However, the assumption that these psychological mechanisms are fully contaminated by the prior acceptance of a repressive authority cannot logically be sustained. The theoretical aim of Freud's account of the Oedipus complex, as Julia Kristeva (1987, pp. 9–10) argues, 'was not, as [Freud] has been too easily accused of, to respect the paternal law of taboos that sketch our social interplay . . . [but rather] to sort out the types of representations of which a subject is capable'. Psychoanalysis does not claim that repressive subjectivity is the fated outcome of all Oedipal struggles. Rather, such distortions and pathologies are but *one* possible outcome of human interactions.

The central deficiency of Marcuse's and Adorno's account of internalization, then, is that it treats human subjectivity as a uniform *object* of an internalized social compulsion. This viewpoint, as we have charted, is based upon the assumption that the subject is closed off in a separate, asocial world until, through the monadic internalization of paternal authority, a repressive self-identity is forged. However, this assumption is only possible if one ignores the fact that processes of identity formation are embedded within specific social contexts of intersubjective relations. Such a recognition that self-identity is constituted through interactive human relationships is of the utmost significance for many reasons. For, as Jessica Benjamin has argued (1990), the function of paternal authority in the Oedipus complex cannot be reduced to a 'model' of power which is simply introjected by the individual subject. Rather, an intersubjective focus highlights the way in which the father can just as easily be a *partner* in forging emotional understanding and empathy. Indeed, it is through the development of interactive identifications that individual autonomy arises. Instead of concentrating solely on the limits that social organization places upon subjectivity, then, Benjamin suggests we should concentrate also on the gains in emotional expression that Oedipal interactions generate. Or, to repeat the Freudian formulation, the constitution of self-identity should be traced as the complicated interplay of independence and dependence, autonomy and heteronomy.

Second, notwithstanding these problems, there is the confusion of the symbolic properties of social relationships with external reality itself in Marcuse's and Adorno's work. By this tendency to merge the nature of the symbolic with the object-world, I refer specifically to the role of the father in the formation of self-identity. As we have seen, Marcuse and Adorno view the decline of the *real father's* social prestige as inevitably bringing with it a disintegration of moral conscience and individual autonomy in the current social order. In psychoanalytic theory, however, the function of paternal authority in the Oedipus complex is principally *symbolic*: to bar the small child's desire towards the mother through introducing the structuring law of social relations, the prohibition of incest. This function, it should be emphasized, is not in any way dependent on the actual social or economic situation of the father. On the contrary: clinical evidence suggests that a 'weak father' (defined as having low self-esteem and autonomy) can actually 'produce' children with excessively strong and sadistic superegos. (For a review of these materials see Held, p. 372.) But the crucial point of significance is that, by reducing the Oedipus complex to a focus on the actual influence of the parents over the subject, Marcuse and Adorno altogether lose sight of the symbolic quality of these human identifications. Accordingly, this is clearly a poor theoretical basis upon which to project such massive cultural transitions in processes of identity-formation.

Third, in fixing the internalization process so fundamentally around the Oedipus complex, Marcuse and Adorno neglect the important psychic processes of the subject's pre-Oedipal development. In doing so, it is clear that much about the psychic paths towards individual autonomy is screened from view. As Melanie Klein's analytic work with children demonstrates so profoundly, the first three to four months of life, prior to the infant's construction of the mother as a whole person, are crucial to a subject's later imaginary space and capacity for rational autonomy (Klein, 1958). Indeed, the progressive valorization of objects from a persecutory stage of good–bad, to a state in which ambivalence can be tolerated, depends on this pre-Oedipal constitution of the ego. Such a standpoint also theorizes in a more thoroughgoing fashion the influence of maternal authority as well as the psychic differences in female child development. In more recent social-theoretical accounts of self-identity, this pre-Oedipal period of development is treated as an essential medium of the way in which cultural practices are created, sustained and changed. In the recent work of Julia Kristeva, for example, these pre-Oedipal configurations of libidinal drives are posited as a basis for both the resistance to social domination, and as a potential springboard for fundamental social change. While it is certainly an open question as to the effects on thought and action of these psychic processes, the failure of Marcuse and Adorno to consider them in any detail is a major deficiency of their account of the evolution of subjectivity.

SUBJECTIVITY, FRAGMENTATION AND CULTURAL MODERNITY

In this final section, I shall make several critical remarks about the implications of Marcuse's and Adorno's work for the interpretation of contemporary culture. A central argument developed by Marcuse and Adorno is that, with the emergence of late capitalism, there are increasing psychic tendencies towards conformity, acceptance and passivity. From this standpoint, as I have emphasized, the more society becomes integrated through instrumental reason and technical rationality, the more severe is the repression of subjectivity. That the conflictual and antagonistic processes of modernity inscribe and reform the psyche in such a one-sided and homogeneous fashion, however, seems a rather simplistic and dubious line of argument. Consider, for example, Marcuse's discussion of the temporal restructuring of the psyche generated by contemporary work practices in late capitalism. Marcuse suggests an interpretation of work processes in modern industrial societies that are entirely structured by the organizational principles of social and bureaucratic domination. As he develops this, it is the routinization and regimentation of the daily labour schedule, the strict adherence to 'clock-time', that gears psychic reality towards a measurable, homogeneous and linear experience of work. Through the repression of libidinal drives and individual spontaneity, modern systems of domination are able to implant a 'happy consciousness' that is practically unopposed by society. But there can be little doubt that Marcuse's analyses of these processes, which are only pointed to in the most general way, are oversimplified and excessively deterministic. Such an analysis leaves no room for the autonomous action of acting subjects, which forms the starting point for the progressive unfolding of social contradictions. Because the burdens of suffering in the workplace are seen as the result of a technical rationality and formalized repression writ large, the actual experiences people have of labour processes and institutional organizations are written off as mere 'delusions of autonomy'.[8] This gives the impression that the connections between social power and the structure of modern work practices affect everyone in an equal manner. It thus completely ignores the intricate ways in which repressive work and industrial relations are produced, sustained and experienced by individuals in various social settings.

These points connect to deeper theoretical difficulties in the work of Marcuse and Adorno. Whatever the fragmentary and dispersed character of modern self-identity, Marcuse and Adorno actually project an image of cultural modernity as an increasingly homogeneous and unified social system – a 'totally administered society'. The reproduction of the political order is viewed as a complex process of 'social incorporation' to the dominant cultural values and institutional arrangements of society. This 'incorporation' is traced as the result of several factors: the manipulation of unconscious processes, the repression of cognition, the disintegration of individual autonomy and so on. Yet the picture of a 'totally administered society' is surely a misleading one in many ways. The social and economic conditions of the advanced capitalist societies over the last fifty or so years, as several commentators have argued, have been far more conflictual and antagonistic than Marcuse's and Adorno's analyses recognize. (See, for example, P. Piccone's introductory criticisms in (eds) Arato and Gebhardt, 1985, pp. xvi ff.) As Anthony Giddens remarks (1982, pp. 154 ff.), this is largely symptomatic of the failure in the first generation of critical theory to accord any real weight to the structural differentiations of late-capitalist society, or to the proliferation of social divisions between its members. This neglect is highly significant since it screens out the performative consequences of specific strategies of political contestation and cultural resistance: of the *conflictual* reproduction of widely differentiated systems of power and forms of oppression and exploitation.

The increasing importance of social movements in modern life perhaps provides something of a baseline here. The struggles of countercultural groups – such as the ecological, peace and feminist movements, as well as the more traditional solidarities of labour associations – all provide a glimpse of the multi-dimensional and contested political character of the modern world. Seeking to secure and advance the rights of political and economic equality, these associations represent a crucial site of collective action against social power and domination. As a mode of political engagement in modern life, social movements highlight the fact that the creative and active dimensions of human subjectivity have not been entirely repressed. Clearly, Marcuse's and Adorno's theory of an intensifying dull conformity, however much it then captured the Cold War mood in American society, is palpably unable to come to grips with many aspects of contemporary social processes.

The foregoing comments on the theory of a 'totally administered society' highlight the way in which Marcuse's and Adorno's analyses are based upon a consensual model of social reproduction. My critical remarks, however, are not intended to suggest that Marcuse and Adorno were themselves ignorant of the objective fragmentations of contemporary capitalist societies. On the contrary, many of their observations demonstrate a keen awareness of these processes. But it is because of the *fractured* character of self-identity, of the split between consciousness and the unconscious, that Marcuse and Adorno invert the existence of social incorporation for modern subjects to dominant institutional arrangements. There is a good deal of recent social research, however, which suggests that the reproduction of the social order is dependent, not so much upon a consensus of collective values, but rather upon subjective and cultural fragmentations and tensions.[9] On this view, dominative relations of cultural production are structured not through a prior ideological incorporation (whether conscious or unconscious), but through the very propagation of social antagonisms and divisions. Yet such antagonisms, precisely because of their fragmented character, are unable to pose any real threat to systems of power within the present system. Rejecting the view that social reproduction operates via a unification of the social field, John Thompson argues this point in the following way:

> oppositional attitudes do not necessarily generate a coherent alternative view which would provide a basis for political action. Hostility and scepticism are often interfused with traditional and conservative values and are commonly tempered by a sense of resignation . . . The reproduction of the social order may depend less upon a consensus with regard to dominant values or norms than upon a *lack of consensus* at the very point where oppositional attitudes could be translated into political action. (1984, p. 63)

This argument can be pressed further on issues of psychic structure. The social divisions and antagonisms that these studies point to are certainly a consequence of human social activity. But it is important to see that these fragmentations and tensions of the ideological field actually 'feed back' into the emotions and desires of individual subjects. Marcuse's and Adorno's contention that it is the fractured quality of self-identity, the split between consciousness and the unconscious, which provides the basis for an *inverse* level of social incorporation, is inadequate. Contemporary social divisions, it can plausibly be argued, are actually *ramified* by unconscious axes – axes which are at once creative productions and yet which already bear the weight of ideology upon them. The unconscious processes of displacement, condensation, distortion and so on significantly deepen and regroove the fundamental social conflicts centred around class, gender and race.[10] The general point is that such divisions and tensions do not operate solely on a sociological plane, but they become inscribed deeply in subjective–unconscious experience. If this is so, this gives an even greater plausibility to the viewpoint that the current social order is reproduced and sustained more through dissensus than through a unification of the ideological field.

Such deficiencies suggest that the thesis of fragmentation is predicated upon assumptions about modernity that all too severely limit the diffuseness of psychic reality. An overemphasis on the homogeneity and cohesion of psychic conformity in modern capitalist societies led the first generation of critical theory to a position in which it was effectively unable to distinguish between different social and ideological formations. Such had become the instrumentalizing dynamic of reification (and its attendant 'corporealization' of the psyche), that individualist patterns of identity-formation had been reduced to a mere façade, to surface phenomena. As a result, at the moment in which a specific analysis is attempted – such as Adorno's studies on the nature of narcissistic identification in particular fascist movements, or Marcuse's appraisals of the nature of totalitarianism – the demonstrated logic all too quickly becomes amalgamated with the content and form of commodified reification and the culture industry.[11]

To be sure, there is a major controversy in much current cultural theory about the alleged ubiquity of psychic fragmentation and narcissism. On the one hand, clinical evidence highlights a dramatic increase in the number of individuals displaying pathological narcissism.[12] This evidence suggests that the nature of such psychic disorders concerns fragmentation anxieties about the unity and intactness of the self. Unable to form relationships with any real emotional commitment, it is said that such personalities often prove socially adaptive by masking such anxieties through grandiose, narcissistic illusions of self-containment. These narcissistic 'illusions' characteristically centre around the pursuit of material success and power. The work of Kernberg (1975) and Kohut (1977), two leading psychoanalytic writers on disturbed narcissism, demonstrates that underneath the narcissist's veneer of social adaptation lie intense feelings of separation and isolation. These feelings can become so intense that they surge into disintegration anxieties and fears of self-annihilation. Other writers have reached much the same conclusion, but connect these feelings of powerlessness more directly to the cultural forms of modern social life. In a major essay on the links between narcissism as a pathogenetic entity and as a sociological trend, Joel Kovel comments that as a result of these modern fragmentations the individual suffers from a kind of emptiness. Experience seems drained and lifeless, without real texture. It is not that things are not perceived sharply – for usually the narcissistic character is if anything hypersensitive – and it is not that correct functioning is impossible – for quite often, the world being what it is, the individual functions at quite a high level. It is rather that, in the zone of felt experience between perception and action, a kind of cold hollowness transpires. (1988, p. 194)

In teasing out the sociological implications of this, Kovel argues that there are a multiplicity of narcissistic forms in modern personal relations. Moreover, he suggests that narcissism plays a substantial psychic role in the fortunes of late-capitalist society. These themes also connect directly to the more popularized writings of Christopher Lasch, who uses such evidence of psychic fragmentation to posit a 'culture of narcissism' (Lasch, 1979). In Lasch's view, modernity signifies the penetration of fragmentation and commodification into the very tissue of the psyche and human social relationships.

On the other hand, the work of an array of authors, such as Jürgen Habermas (1987), Jessica Benjamin (1990) and Joel Whitebook (1985), suggests that the fabric of modern personal relations has not been normalized and fragmented in this way. While there is by no means a consensus of opinion among these authors, there is the theoretical insistence in their work that the transition to modern forms of personal relations contains the *possibility* of new modalities of self-actualization and individual autonomy. Alert to the repressive, narcissistic and instrumental aspects of modern social life, these writers, in divergent ways, also stress the gains in freedom and expressive possibilities which flow from mutual interaction. Accordingly, for these commentators, modernity exhibits a series of ambivalent tendencies for the future of human social relationships. What such standpoints suggest is that it is possible to acknowledge the psychic costs caused by capitalist development, without concluding that subjective fragmentation is the inevitable fate of humankind. For Habermas, who wants to defend the 'project of modernity' against the analysis of the self-negating character of reason, it is this totalizing critique of cultural reification by Marcuse and Adorno which most blurs the contours of self-identity in modernity. As he remarks, the critical theorists

> detach the concept of reification not only from the special historical context of the rise of the capitalist economic system but from the dimension of interhuman relations altogether; and they generalize it temporally (over the entire history of the human species) and substantively (the same logic of domination is imputed to both cognition in the service of self-preservation and the repression of instinctual nature). This double generalization of the concept of reification leads to a concept of instrumental reason that shifts the primordial history of subjectivity and the self-formative process of ego-identity into an encompassing historic-philosophical perspective. (1984, p. 382)

It is not my purpose here to insist on the priority of either of these competing interpretations of modern identity, nor to seek to attempt some sort of reconciliation between them. Like all terrains of subjectivity, the situation is assuredly more subtle and complex. I do not think it justifiable, however, to see the phenomena that Marcuse and Adorno analyse as showing the power of capitalist modernity to empty out the human subject of all personal identity and feeling, as draining whatever was left of ego substance and psychic interiority. Though the thesis of psychic fragmentation has undeniably served to discredit the influence of liberal notions of an autonomous subject, it would appear that there are a number of obscurities that attend any attempt to assess the concretization of this doctrine in contemporary social processes. It may well be that, at present, it is not possible, or even desirable, to separate the gains from the losses here. That is, whatever the actual impact of the fragmentation of subjectivity, it is extraordinarily difficult to work out whether these changes merely reflect the lived experience of modernity or whether they suggest the development of new, alternative processes of subjectivity. But a more plausible interpretation might be that contemporary social development in some sense intersects with a subjectivity torn with psychic ambivalences – between unity and fragmentation, hope and despair.

NOTES

1 For a general discussion of the integration of psychoanalysis into the theoretical work of the first generation of critical theory, see Jay, 1973, ch. 3; Held, 1980, ch. 4.

2 For a review of the concept of the 'totally administered world' and 'administered subject' as the common denominator in the theoretical works of Marcuse and Adorno, see Honneth, 1987, pp. 371ff.

3 Cf. Marcuse's 'Critique of neo-Freudian revisionism', printed as the epilogue of *Eros and Civilization*, pp. 238–74.

4 See Adorno, 1955b. References in this study are to the English translation by Irving N. Wohlfarth, 'Sociology and psychology' (Adorno, 1967); Adorno, 1951; Adorno, 1955a.

5 The following overview refers, in particular, to Adorno's account of the dialectic of the 'ego and non-ego', 'Sociology and psychology' (1967, pp. 67ff.).

6 Lacan's distinction highlights the point that biological needs have no *determining* role in processes of repression. For example, it clearly allows us to comprehend the difficulties in Freud's interpretation of the connections between biological needs and libidinal drives in the following passage from his *New Introductory Lectures*:

> The sexual drives are noticeable to us for their plasticity, their capacity for altering their aims, their replaceability . . . and their readiness for being deferred . . . We should be glad to deny these characteristics to the self-preservative drives, and to say of them that they are inflexible, admit of no delay, are imperative in a very different sense and have a quite other relationship to repression and anxiety. But a little reflection tells us that this exceptional position applies, not to all ego drives, but only to hunger and thirst, and is evidently based on a peculiar character of the sources of these drives. (1933, p. 97)

Freud's confusions about the place of the functions of self-preservation are particularly evident. In contrast to the sexual drives – which because of their plasticity are unconscious *desires* – the forces of hunger and thirst, in Lacan's scheme, are classified as biological *needs*, due to their instinctual rigidity. Such needs, however, play no *determining* part in the specific social-historical structuring of the representational process or of the specific configurations of repression.

Against Marcuse and Adorno, this is properly the *creative* place of unconscious desire. A fuller treatment of these issues is Wilden, 1969, pp. 216ff.; 1973.

7 The results of such research are summarized in Giddens, 1984, pp. 239–42. The following paragraphs draw directly on Giddens' arguments that social theory should avoid postulating such homologies between the increasing complexity of social life on the one hand and intensified levels of psychological repression on the other.

8 For a discussion of the deficiencies of Marcuse's account of the institutional processes of social reproduction see Offe, 1988.

9 The sociological research which highlights the pervasiveness of social differentiation and fragmentation has been extensively developed; here I refer only to the most important texts. Such findings were initially reported in Mann, 1970, 1973. A more recent theorization of these complex interconnections between social differentiation and the ideological field is Thompson, 1984.

10 A useful discussion of the effect of unconscious mechanisms upon the social divisions and tensions of race and gender is Frosh, 1989, chs 4 and 5.

11 The collapsing of distinct social formations, such as the specificity of fascism of Nazi Germany into the content and structure of the 'culture industry' in the US in the 1940s and '50s is particularly evident in Adorno, 1951. For a critique of these shortcomings see Piccone 1976. For a splendid, but neglected, analysis of the subjectivity of fascism which builds upon the work of Adorno, see Hughes, 1975.

12 A useful overview on this evidence is given in *Telos'* 1980 symposium on narcissism and contemporary social processes.

REFERENCES

Adorno, T. (1951) 'Freudian theory and the pattern of fascist propaganda', in Arato and Gebhardt, eds (1985), pp. 118–37.

—— (1955a) 'Die revidierte Psychanalyse' ['Revisionist psychoanalysis'], *Soziologische Schriften*, pt 1, GS, vol. 8, pp. 20–41.

—— (1955b) 'Zum Verhaltnis von Soziologie und Psychologie', *Soziologische Schriften*, pt 1, GS, vol. 8.

—— (1967) 'Sociology and psychology' [trans. of Adorno, 1955b], *New Left Review*, 46: 67–80.

—— (1973) *Negative Dialectics*, E.B. Ashton, trans. New York: Continuum.

Arato, A. and Gebhardt, E. (eds) (1985) *The Essential Frankfurt School Reader*. New York: Continuum.

Benjamin, J. (1990) *The Bonds of Love: Psychoanalysis, Feminism and the Problem of Domination*. London: Virago.

Deleuze, G. and Guattari, F. (1977) *Anti-Oedipus*. New York: Viking.

Dews, P. (1987) *Logics of Disintegration: Post-Structuralist Thought and the Claims of Critical Theory*. London: Verso.

Freud, S. (1933) *New Introductory Lectures on Psycho-Analysis*, in James Strachey, ed. *The Standard Edition of the Complete Psychological Works of Sigmund Freud*, 24 vols. London: Hogarth, 1953–73, vol. 22, pp. 1–182.

Frosh, S. (1989) *Psychoanalysis and Psychology: Minding the Gap*. London: Macmillan.

Giddens, A. (1982) *Profiles and Critiques in Social Theory*. London: Macmillan.

—— (1984) *The Constitution of Society*. Cambridge: Polity Press.

Habermas, J. (1984) *The Theory of Communicative Action*, vol. 1, *Reason and the Rationalization of Society*. Cambridge: Polity Press.

—— (1987) *The Philosophical Discourse of Modernity*. Cambridge: Polity Press.

Held, D. (1980) *Introduction to Critical Theory*. London: Hutchinson.

Honneth, A. (1987) 'Critical theory', in A. Giddens and J.H. Turner, eds *Social Theory Today*. Cambridge: Polity Press.

Horkheimer, M. and Adorno, T.W. (1973) *Dialectic of Enlightenment*. London: Allen Lane, 1975.

Hughes, A. (1975) *Psychology and the Political Experience*. Cambridge: Cambridge University Press.

Jameson, F. (1988) *The Ideologies of Theory*, vol. 1, *Situations of Theory*. London: Routledge.

Jay, M. (1973) *The Dialectical Imagination*. Boston: Little, Brown.

—— (1984) *Adorno*. London: Fontana.

Kernberg, O.F. (1975) *Borderline Conditions and Pathological Narcissism*. New York: Jason Aronson.

Klein, M. (1958) 'On the development of mental functioning', in *Envy and Gratitude and Other Works*. London: Virago, 1988, pp. 236–46.

Kohut, H. (1977) *The Restoration of the Self*. New York: International Universities Press.

Kovel, J. (1988) *The Radical Spirit: Essays on Psychoanalysis and Society*. London: Free Association Books.

Kristeva, J. (1988) *Tales of Love*. New York: Columbia University Press.

Laplanche, J. (1969) 'Notes sur Marcuse et la psychanalyse', *La Nef* 26, Cahier no. 36.

Laplanche, J. and Pontalis, J.-B. (1973) *The Language of Psychoanalysis*. London: Hogarth/Institute of Psycho-Analysis.

Lasch, C. (1979) *The Culture of Narcissism*. London: Abacus.

Mann, M. (1970) 'The social cohesion of liberal democracy', *American Sociological Review* 35: 423–39.

—— (1973) *Consciousness and Action among the Western Working Class*. London: Macmillan.

Marcuse, H. (1956) *Eros and Civilization: A Philosophical Inquiry into Freud*. London: Ark.

—— (1966) *One-Dimensional Man: Studies in Advanced Industrial Society*. Boston, MA: Beacon.

—— (1970) *Five Lectures: Psychoanalysis, Politics and Utopia*. London: Allen Lane.

Offe, C. (1988) 'Technology and one-dimensionality: a version of the technocracy thesis?', in R. Pippin, A. Feenberg and C. Webel, eds *Marcuse: Critical Theory and the Promise of Utopia*. London: Macmillan, pp. 215–24.

Piccone, P. (1976) 'From tragedy to farce: the return of critical theory', *New German Critique* 7: 91–105.

Telos (1980) 'Symposium on narcissism', no. 44, pp. 88–101.

Thompson, J.B. (1984) *Studies in the Theory of Ideology*. Cambridge: Polity Press.

Whitebook, J. (1985) 'Reason and happiness: some psychoanalytic themes in critical theory', in R.J. Bernstein, ed. *Habermas and Modernity*. Cambridge: Polity Press, pp. 140–60.

Wilden, A. (1969) 'Marcuse and the Freudian model: energy, information and phantasie', *Salmagundi* no. 10/11, pp. 196–245.

—— (1973) *System and Structure*. London: Tavistock.

Address for correspondence: Department of Political Science, University of Melbourne, Parkville, Victoria 3052, Australia

DEBATE

The mirror and the hammer: depth psychology and political transformation

Andrew Samuels

INTRODUCTION

The paper is about the depth psychology of political processes, focusing on processes of political change. It is a contribution to the longstanding ambition of depth psychology to develop a form of political and cultural analysis that will, in Freud's words, 'understand the riddles of the world'. It has to be admitted that there is an equally longstanding reluctance in the non-psychological community to accept the many and varied ideas and suggestions concerning political matters that have been offered by analysts of all persuasions. I do not believe this can all be put down to resistance. There is something offensive above reductive interpretations of complex socio-political problems in exclusively psychological terms. The tendency to panpsychism on the part of some depth psychologists has led me to wonder if an adequate methodology and ethos actually exists with which to make an engagement of depth psychology with the public sphere possible.

By 'politics' I mean the arrangements within a culture for the organization and distribution of power, especially economic power, and the way in which power is deployed to maintain the survival

Free Associations (1993) Volume 3, Part 4 (No. 28): 545–93

and enhance the quality of human life. Economic and political power includes control of processes of information and representation as well as the use of physical force and possession of vital resources such as land, food and water. On a more personal level, political power reflects the ability to choose freely whether to act and what action to take in a given situation. 'Politics' refers to the interplay between the personal and public dimensions of power. That is, there is an articulation between public, economic power and power as expressed on the personal, private level. This articulation is demonstrated in family organization, gender and race relations, and in religious and artistic assumptions as they affect the life of individuals. (I have also tried to be consistent in my use of the terms 'culture', 'society' and 'collective'.)[1]

Here is an example of the difficulty with psychological reductionism to which I am referring. At a conference I attended in London in 1990, a distinguished psychoanalyst referred to the revolutionary students in Paris in 1968 as 'functioning as a regressive group'. Now, for a large group of students to be said to regress, there must be, in the speaker's mind, some sort of normative developmental starting point for them to regress to. The social group is supposed to have a babyhood, as it were. Similarly, the speaker must have had in mind the possibility of a healthier, progressive group process – what a more mature group of revolutionary students would have looked like. But complex social and political phenomena do not conform to the individualistic, chronological, moralistic, pathologizing framework that is often imported.

The problem stems from treating the entire culture, or large chunks of it, as if it were an individual or, worse, as if it were a baby. Psychoanalysts project a version of personality development couched in judgemental terms onto a collective cultural and political process. If we look in this manner for pathology in the culture, we will surely find it. As we are looking with a psychological theory in mind, then, lo and behold, the theory will explain the pathology. But this is a retrospective prophecy (to use a phrase of Freud's), twenty–twenty hindsight. In this psychoanalytic tautologizing there is really nothing much to get excited about. Too much psychological writing on the culture, my own included, has suffered from this kind of smug 'correctness' when the 'material' proves the theoretical point. Of course it does! If we are interested in envy or greed, then we will find envy or greed in capitalistic organization. If we set out to demonstrate the presence of archetypal patterns, such as projection of the shadow, in geopolitical relations, then, without a doubt, they will seem to leap out at us. We influence what we analyse and so psychological reflection on culture and politics needs to be muted; there is not so much 'aha!' as one hoped.

Depth psychology concerns a person's subjective experience of social and cultural structures, and that is valuable in itself. But I want to ask: is there a special psychology of and for politics and culture? If so, what does the clinical practice of analysis and therapy with individuals or small groups contribute to the forming of such a psychology? And, conversely, I ask: what does a perspective taken from cultural or political analysis contribute to a clinical analysis of an individual or small group? In what way is the personal political – and in what way is the political personal?

I am sure that this paper and the book of which it is to be a part (Samuels, 1993, forthcoming) cannot solve all these problems or answer all these questions. My title is adapted from some lines by the Russian Futurist poet Vladimir Mayakovsky, written in the 1920s: 'Art is not a mirror to reflect the world, but a hammer with which to shape it'. I think depth psychology has to do both; as part of a multi-disciplinary project, and in a mixture of styles ranging from exegetical sobriety, to playfulness, to something frankly irrational.

BEZALEEL'S BOX: PSYCHE, CULTURE AND RESACRALIZATION

It has never been more difficult to make a psychological analysis of culture for, in our day, every element of culture is undergoing fragmentation and Balkanization. It has become harder and harder to see what, if anything, holds culture together. Moments at which one apprehends a social or personal oneness, revelatory and mystical moments, have become rather precious and vulnerable.

I want to take the anxiety-provoking ideas of fragmentation, fracture and complexity, and imagine them as the tools of the trade of psychological analysis of processes of political change. Let us take fragmentation, fracture and complexity as *healing* as well as wounding to a sense of political and social empowerment. My suggestion is that amidst the tragic anomie and baffling atomization; amidst the dreadful conformism of 'international' architecture, telecommunications and cuisine; amidst the sense of oppression and fear of a horrific future, an equally fragmented, fractured and complex attempt at a resacralization of the culture is going on. There are many surface signs of resacralization: New Age or New Times thought, expressing concern for the quality of life, green politics, feminism, the human potential movement, finding God in the new physics.

I would even include trying to engage depth psychology with politics and the culture on this list; I certainly do not want to leave myself out. Analysts concerned with the public sphere have not paid much attention to themselves as a cultural phenomenon. In fairness, I do not assume that only left-leaning, so-called progressive political and religious movements partake in resacralization. Born-again Christians and other fundamentalists are part of the trend. In different forms, of course, resacralization is also a way to describe what has been happening in Eastern Europe and the former Soviet Union.

As I said, I think all these are surface signs that something deeper is going on. I want to depict resacralization as a contemporary attempt to shift a sense of holiness into the secular and material world. Let's look at holiness. The roots of holiness do not only lie in God or in a transpersonal realm. They also lie in humanity's *making* of holiness. We make holiness by the designation and construction of sacred spaces (which we call temples). We make holiness by the performance of sacred acts (such as sacrifice and repentance). I doubt that contemporary resacralization will ultimately glorify God or lead to a new religion. But, along the way, most aspects of human culture will be touched by this attempt to connect to a feeling level that we sense once existed but we find has vanished from the modern world (hence *re*sacralization). I think that this involves more than a search for a new (and better) ethical basis for society.

The notion that holiness is located in the material world is not a new one. For many, religious and non-religious alike, the world has long held a Chassidic gleam. Since my childhood, I have been fascinated by God's detailed instructions to the Children of Israel about how to build the Ark of the Covenant (not to mention the Tabernacle, or, earlier, Noah's Ark). In the divine detail of the construction, we see how ineffable holiness depends on every single joint, bevel, dimension, and the material used:

> And Bezaleel made the ark of shittim wood: two cubits and a half was the length of it, and a cubit and a half the breadth of it, and a cubit and a half the height of it. And he overlaid it with pure gold within and without, and made a crown of gold to it round about. And he cast for it four rings of gold, to be set by the four corners of it; even two rings upon the one side of it, and two rings upon the other side of it. And he made staves of shittim wood, and overlaid them with gold. And he put the staves into the rings by the side of the ark, to bear the ark. (Exod. 37: 1–5)

Bezaleel's name is hardly ever mentioned, not even in the film *Raiders of the Lost Ark*! Yet he is the collective image and cultural personification of resacralization, the contemporary drive to render the secular holy.

For many, resacralization has meant a return to religion. Sometimes this is established religion, sometimes archaic (or apparently archaic) religion. As a psychologist, I travel in another direction. I try to pick up on what I think is going on. I try to make something psychological, but not exclusively psychological, out of a host of specific cultural impressions. The idea is to bring something up and out that is already there – so these words of mine about resacralization are intended to be description, chronicle and interpretation, not sermon or advocacy.

One specific impression is of a growing, collective sense of disgust, in both Western culture and the once-communist states, for the world in whose making we have participated. Disgust is lurking alongside the shallowness and cruelty of much of modern life; our subjectivity is full of it. Disgust with our present politics leads us to aspire to a reformed politics led, perhaps, by a new psychological valuing of the potential of political engagement itself. Involvement in the external world and passionate political involvement are as psychologically valuable as an interior perspective. Just as politics can be a means of avoiding personal conflicts or acting out such conflicts, so it can surely also be a means of expressing what is best in humans, acknowledging the fact of our social being, that we are not the isolated, solipsistic monads that some psychological theories might lead us to believe (Paul Gordon, personal communication, 1990).

A more evolved attitude to politics is something to work on in the consulting room, just as we work on more evolved attitudes to sexuality and aggression. Later on, I shall propose that we begin to work out a model that enables us to refer to a person's *political drive*, to his or her level of *political development*, and to a *political level of the psyche*. In clinical practice, such a model would enable us to generate new readings of personal and collective *political imagery*. We may even find that there is a *politics of imagery*. Political imagery will be as fluid and unpredictable in its display of what is positive and negative in the individual and in the culture as any other kind of imagery, for not all political imagery presents the worst case for humanity.

Our culture (and not just our culture) is longing to atone for its injustices and the sense of disgust it feels for them, longing to be able to think good thoughts about itself and rid itself of depressive preoccupation with its own destructiveness. We are already full of guilty contempt for capitalism (and for what passed for socialism in the East). But there is a lack of any ritual by which we could make repentance on a cultural scale. Lacking ritual and a symbolic language with which to express our unease and disgust, and our desire to atone, we make a split between the constructive and the cheating sides of capitalism and the market economy, preferring to see and hence to support only one side or the other.

On the negative side, we have chiliast fantasies of an apocalyptic end, whether by nuclear conflagration, AIDS pandemic, or the greenhouse effect. Certainly, these anxieties are rooted in reality. But taken as fantasies, they are the deepest signs of our own self-punishing contempt for ourselves. We think we deserve to perish like this. We may even wish it. On the positive side, we tend to extol capitalism as the source of the material benefits that we enjoy today and as the only economic system that seems to work.

We can see this negative/positive split very clearly in relation to the market economy. Is the market economy a socially divisive rich man's charter, as even supporters of it in Britain or the United States are beginning to say? Or is the market economy the road to freedom and dignity as many in Eastern Europe and the former Soviet Union now seem to think? Or is it the best available compromise? Or – and this is the line I intend to take – is it both a negative and a positive phenomenon *at the same time*, with the negative and positive verdicts each having a distinct psychology of its own that resists compromise? In this way of looking at the market economy, not only are our negative and positive images of it not split off from each other, but they each guarantee the existence of the other; there will be no chance of realizing the positive features of the market economy *without* accepting the *simultaneous* presence of the negative features of the market economy. It is relatively easy to reject the Manichean, crude, psychologically primitive, split approach in which the market must be good or bad. But the approach that attempts a balanced view of the market is almost as problematic, psychologically speaking. In the 'balanced' approach, there is a difficulty in incorporating the undoubtedly unfair and ruthless features of free market economies and of seeing how they *have to be present* for the benefits of the market to be available. They are not unfortunate by-products of the market; according to this psychological analysis, they are its *sine qua non* and cannot be ameliorated.

Our inability to stay in emotional contact with the psychologically distinct and separate images of the market makes it difficult to address the psychological issues that are central to notions of economic and political change. I am sure that *economics* should be the psychological focus and, later, in order to concentrate on splits within the image of the market economy, I will enlist the aid of the myth of Hermes to help us to hold on to both sides, positive and negative, of our evaluation of the market economy. Many if not most would agree that there are (at least) two sides to the question of the market economy. My point is that Hermes can provide a base for an approach that avoids the twin dangers of splitting and of trying to reach a supposedly 'balanced' view. To the extent that there are opposite feelings in the air about the market, it is very hard, emotionally, to hold on to these as necessarily existing opposites without having recourse to either a schizoid judgemental retreat or to glib sloganizing about accepting the bad with the good in a supposedly balanced synthesis. We need to know more about the psychology of the market as a positive phenomenon *and* about the psychology of the market as a negative phenomenon. Then, perhaps, we could attempt to work out the psychology of the market without the introduction of the categories 'positive' and 'negative'.

For the moment, we do have to let 'positive' and 'negative' structure our psychological response to market economics. But there is a hidden gain in this. For maintaining an attitude of evaluation and judgement enables us to see to what extent the preceding ideas about attitudes to and images of the market are relevant outside Western, capitalistic culture.

It seems as if the *Zeitgeist* in the former Soviet Union and Eastern Europe is quite different from that of the West. In the West, criticisms of the excesses of free market economics are beginning to surface in circles that had, hitherto, been gung-ho for the market. For example, it seems that the long sentence passed on Michael Milken, the 'junk bond king', was 'widely seen as public retribution for the excesses of the '80s' and resulted from 'public anger over the ethics of the age', according to *The Times* of 22 November 1990. Kevin Phillips, a one-time senior aide of President Reagan, published a bestselling book in 1990 entitled *The Politics of Rich and Poor* which prophesied the end of an ethical and political climate that permitted 'the triumph of upper America – an ostentatious celebration of wealth, the political ascendancy of the richest third of the population and a glorification of capitalism, free markets and finance' (Phillips, 1990, p. xvii).

In the East, things seem to be going the other way. The free market is hailed not only as the sole means to revive moribund economies, but also as a means to a spiritual revival. However, I wonder if the two completely different political situations do not share some psychological features in common. Both societies are fascinated, even obsessed by the market; the one eager now to condemn it, the other to praise and implement it. Both have the same difficulty in getting beyond a verdict that is either good or bad. Both seem to sense the limitations of the 'balanced' view and we see this in the former Soviet Union in the popular rejection of Gorbachev's idea of a 'third way' incorporating what is best in communism and capitalism, and in the United States in the almost total disagreement about what can be done to ease the plight of the so-called underclass (including intense argument over whether such a grouping actually exists). Crucially, in both West and East, modes of economic and political organization are seen nowadays as inseparable from psychological, ethical and spiritual themes. One Russian commentator had this to say: 'the main thing is for people to learn to be human. If we have bread and still become beasts, there will be no reason for us to live' (quoted in the *Spectator*, 29 September 1990).

The idea that surface differences between Western and Eastern images and attitudes mask a deeper, psychological similarity is shown dramatically in the play *Moscow Gold*, performed in London and, for one night only, in Moscow, in 1990 (Ali and Brenton, 1990). The play shows the difficulties faced by Gorbachev and his colleagues in deciding what sort of economic organization to aim for. Gorbachev's real-life rival Yeltsin is given the role of supporter of a total and instant adoption of free market economics, in contrast to Gorbachev's more cautious approach. Towards the end of the play, Gorbachev and Yeltsin confront each other under the gaze of the play's Chorus of three Kremlin cleaning women:

Yeltsin: Have you fixed the date for our first ever general election?
Gorbachev: Have you decided on the name of your new party? Christian Democrats? Russian Orthodox Christian Democrats?

Free Market Democrats? National Socialist Russian Memory Party?

Yeltsin [smiling]: I love it when you're scared.

They both smile. Yeltsin offers a hand. Gorbachev offers his.

We are on the same side you know. It's me you need. Not the dead forces. Together we could transform this country. Russia alone could become a paradise. The California of Europe.

Their hands freeze and fall.

Gorbachev: Look. There goes your mouth again, Boris. We must have no illusions about the free market. There will be social explosions if we put fifteen million people out of work.

Yeltsin: People would accept temporary unemployment *if* they trust the leadership.

Gorbachev [a flash of anger]: Don't you have any sense of the dangers involved? What if the people don't accept it? Will you give our soldiers the order to open fire on millions of workers rioting for jobs?

Zoya, Lena and Katya now move to the centre of the stage pushing the two men apart, and occupy that position.

Yeltsin: Let's ask them.

Zoya: My flat's been sold. I wake up one morning and find that I've got a new landlady. Is this perestroika?

Yeltsin: Tell me Zoya – are you in favour of the free market?

Zoya: Yes!

Gorbachev: Are you in favour of everyone's right to work?

All three: Yes!

Yeltsin: Are you in favour of greater wealth in this country?

Zoya: Yes!

Gorbachev: And in favour of a new middle class, fifty times better off than you?

The three women look at each other. Then angrily:

Zoya: No!

Katya: No!

Lena: No!

The two men look at each other in silence.

THE LION AND THE FOX: MORALITY, TRICKSTER AND POLITICAL CHANGE

Earlier, I mentioned the importance of paying attention to political imagery. After these opening remarks about resacralization and the market economy, I want now to attempt a psychological analysis of the imagery in the political thought of Niccolò Machiavelli. The idea is to explore what an engagement with politics does to psychology and what psychology can bring to political theorizing.

In Machiavelli's short book *The Prince*, written in 1513–14, we find a psychological analysis of the political process. Machiavelli blends wanton subversiveness, subtly buried morality, and relentless imagination. It is possible for us to encounter his encounter with the political culture of his time, seeing 'the prince' as a metaphor for a certain kind of political psychology, or psychological approach to politics.

We can make psychology in a Machiavellian way, think Machiavellian thoughts, see with a Machiavellian eye. The opprobrium heaped on Machiavelli's head for nearly 500 years is also something to muse about. Depth psychologists, such as Freud or Jung, also stir up similar reactions when they bring their psychological theories to bear on the political and social scene. As with Machiavelli's writings, what depth psychologists have to say often appears to subvert every generally held decency. But it is the peculiar quality of the subversiveness found in an apparently reactionary thinker that is the compelling quality in Machiavelli's writings. The subversiveness is not contrived or adolescent, but argued out rather logically.

In *The Prince* Machiavelli completely rejects the four cardinal virtues of wisdom, courage, justice and moderation. In Machiavelli's words:

A prince is forced to know how to act like a beast. He should learn from the fox and the lion; because the lion is defenceless against traps and a fox is defenceless against wolves. Therefore one must be a fox in order to recognize traps, and a lion to frighten off wolves. Those who simply act like lions are stupid . . . Those who have known best how to imitate the fox have come off best. But one must know how to colour one's actions and to be a great liar and deceiver. (Chapter 18)

In spite of statements like this, a conception of morality is not missing from Machiavelli's outlook. The Prince's morality should, above all, be of a flexible nature; he is required to *choose* to be evil, to be evil in spite of himself: 'He should not deviate from what is good, if that is possible, but he should know how to do evil, if that is necessary' (Chapter 18). In modern psychological language, what Machiavelli is doing is to make a morality, and then an ideology, out of the shadow, out of those aspects of human psychology that we would rather disown. Most political theory seeks to combat and deal with the shadow. Machiavelli's approach is to embrace the shadow and go *with* its energies rather than *against* them.

Machiavelli's angle on morality leads us to the legendary figure of the Trickster for, at the same time as being bad, the Prince must *not* appear to be bad:

A prince should be so prudent that he knows how to escape an evil reputation. To those seeing and hearing him, he should appear a man of compassion, a man of good faith, a man of integrity, a kind and religious man . . . Everyone sees what you appear to be, few experience what you really are. (Chapter 18)

It's a trick, you see.

Perhaps it needs to be made clear that this is not Satanic, not Machiavelli taking evil as his good, nor foul as fair. This trickster-ism is *political* – and, by exploring the psychology of Trickster, I intend to test out Machiavelli's insight about the Trickster and politics. The aim is to gain a deeper understanding of the psychology of political process in general and the psychology of political change in particular.

Trickster figures and stories appear in many cultures, as has only quite recently become accepted. For the Greeks, the arch trickster was Hermes, with his tendencies to play jokes, to lie, to cheat, to steal, to deny reality, and to engage in grandiose fantasy. We will meet up with Hermes in a moment. Tricksters generally follow that pattern, undermining the prevailing organization of power and even the perceived structure of reality itself. They can be seen as personifications of primary process activity, disregarding the laws of time, space and place. But they do this *precisely to test the limits of those laws*, the bounds of their applicability and, hence, the possibility of altering them. In the Middle Ages, carnivals began to take their present form and there would usually be a portrayal of some disturbance in the social hierarchy. For example, an unsuitable person, such as a child or the village idiot, would be dressed up as the bishop. In fairy tales, we find figures like Tom Thumb, parodying our usual conception of the hero. Parapsychology is full of tricky poltergeists who strain the boundaries of reality by living out the dramas of the unconscious itself.

One of the most studied Trickster stories is the Trickster Cycle of the North American Winnebago Indians, brought together by Paul Radin in 1956. The Winnebago Trickster lacks even rudimentary body unity: his intestines are outside his body, his penis is autonomous, enormously long, sometimes kept in a box, sometimes wrapped round his abdomen; each hand regards the other as a mortal enemy (like Dr Strangelove, in Kubrick's film).

One episode of the Winnebago Trickster Cycle will illustrate the picaresque kind of thing that happens. Trickster has sent his penis into a tree to punish a chipmunk who has been teasing him. When he withdraws, he finds that only a small piece of the penis is left. He gets hold of the chipmunk and tears him open:

> There, to his horror, he discovered his penis all gnawed up. 'Oh, my, of what a wonderful organ he has deprived me! But why do I speak thus? I will make objects out of the pieces for human beings to use.' Then he took the end of his penis, the part that has no foreskin, and declared, 'This is what human beings will call lily-of-the-lake.' This he threw in a lake nearby. Then he took the other pieces declaring in turn: 'This the people will call potatoes; this the people will call turnips; this the people will call artichokes; this the people will call ground-beans; . . . this the people will call rice.' All these pieces he threw into the water. Finally he took the end of his penis and declared, 'This the people will call the pond-lily.' He was referring to the square part of the end of his penis.

What was left of his penis was not very long. When, at last, he started off again, he left behind the box in which he had until then kept his penis coiled up.

And this is the reason our penis has its present shape. It is because of these happenings that the penis is short. Had the chipmunk not gnawed off Trickster's penis our penis would have the penis that Trickster's first had. It was so large that he had to carry it on his back. Now it would not have been good that our penis remained like that and the chipmunk was created for the precise purpose of performing this particular act. Thus is it said. (1956, pp. 39–40)

Well – is Trickster really the creator of lilies, potatoes and so on? Or is he the creator only of an illusion that he is? Is he a kind of Adam, an original man, whose morphology determined ours? Or is he the prototype of the infant, who has to work out a fantastic explanation of the origins and limitations of the body which he or she inhabits?

Given the secretly normative nature of depth psychology, the Trickster often gets a bad press as symbolizing the anti-social personality (just as Machiavelli has hardly had a good word said about him). Trickster's mendaciousness and self-deception are placed in the foreground, obscuring his transformative and generative aspects and, in particular, the way in which Trickster acts as a sort of yardstick and spur to consciousness.

Considering the Winnebago Trickster Cycle from a conventional psychodynamic angle, the main themes seem to be the absence of a coherent body schema (the mobile penis), projection and splitting (for example, of aggression into the chipmunk), and pathological grandiosity (Trickster as Creator). However, if we recover our sense of humour and suspend judgement for the moment, then these themes lead to certain questions which have a political flavour.

Do the erotogenic zones ever constitute a fixed body schema? Human sexual attraction seems to rest on the interdependence and even interchangeability of the zones: a kiss on the mouth, a cute bottom of either sex, big breasts, a well-stuffed wallet. Similarly, is a split object always so pathological? I wonder whether it is always necessary (or desirable) for splits to be healed, for loving and aggressive impulses to be brought together as psychodynamic theory usually suggests? Or is Trickster's so-called primitive fantasy of a split-off object worthy of positive consideration? Finally, what about Trickster's grandiosity? After Kohut's re-valuing of grandiosity (1971, 1977), how can grandiosity be omitted from any account of human creativity?

These psychological questions are of interest to psychologists for they contribute to a revision of what constitutes maturity. But, as suggested earlier, there is a political reading to be made of these matters. For, in revaluing the Trickster, we revalue Tricksterish politics, maybe even revalue politics itself. These apparently psychological questions about body schema, projection and split-ting, and grandiosity have themselves had major *political* consequences in our own time. If the bodily zones are muddled, then no established order is safe, anything can be muddled: the personal can be political, gender rules reversed, tyranny challenged (if not always overthrown). If love and hate do not always have to be linked in so-called healthy ambivalence then community spirit and ruthless selfishness do not have to cancel each other out. Rather, they engage in an unending struggle for the ruling position. If grandiosity is respected, then what is condemned by the *senex* as a *puer*-like fantasy of a global solution to the world's problems can be reframed as a potentially practical political tool. We can see that it is not really the grandiosity of such solutions that is the only problem, as is often thought; it is *lack* of grandiosity that makes for political compliance. Watching the Romanian uprising on TV in December 1989 (which is when I wrote the first draft of this paper) and seeing unarmed workers and students refuse to leave the streets, getting shot while the army fought the Securitate, drove the point home: that grandiosity of aim can be the healthy ground of realizable ambition. Unhappily, the Romanian people will have further need of their grandiose courage. Trickster's denial of mortality is a political statement, for the fear of death plays a part in maintaining the political *status quo*; it is feared that any change will lead to the total elimination of life itself.

I am arguing that Trickster should not be omitted from a psychology of the political. The Trickster is compatible with order and organization on the one hand and with chaos and fluidity on the other. But Trickster's order is created through chaos; his stabilizing influence on human culture (lilies, potatoes) is an outcrop of his destabilizing influence. What is more, as Beebe has pointed out, we should be very careful about not trusting Trickster (1981, p. 39). If we don't trust him, then he will trick us in an unexpected way, turning out to be absolutely worthy of trust.

We should not look to the Trickster for signs of individuation, achievement of the depressive position, maintenance of firm boundaries, or consistency. But I am trying to develop a depth psychology of politics in which we are not hamstrung by rigid orthodoxies. We tend to accept without question that what seems the most mature will turn out to be the most true. Trickster challenges this assumption. Nevertheless, many may want to know whether a political apprehension of Trickster means that anything goes in politics, that every view should be given equal weight, that political tolerance should be infinite, that there is no political morality.

I think that political morality incorporates a ceaseless dynamic between a passionately expressed, codified, legally sanctioned set of principles and certitudes – and a more open, flexible, improvised, tolerant kind of morality that is basically code-free. These two aspects of political morality are both present in a political system and it is important to resist the temptation to see one of them as somehow more advanced, rising from the ashes of the other. Certitude and improvisation are equally valuable and, even assessed from a developmental perspective, equally mature. It is easy to see that a political morality based exclusively on the Trickster and on improvisation would be too slippery by far and would contribute to a climate in which anything goes. But a political morality based exclusively on principle, law and certitude would be equally problematic (equally 'primitive'). To begin with, laws are not politically effective on their own; legal codes reflect and depend on the distribution of wealth and power. Moreover, political principle easily becomes ossified and used to gain control over others. Finally, codified political and moral prohibitions do not always work, as the prevalence of theft or adultery demonstrates.

Trickster is not unaware of the existence of moral and political certitudes, but these do not constitute his particular political trajectory. Even if orthodox political and moral principles are the windmills against which Trickster tilts, he does not deny them their existence as he tries to undermine them. Can the serious, respectable world of economic, political, and psychological theory and organization extend the same emotionally complex generosity towards the Trickster? Later in the paper, I shall continue to explore the consequences of a challenge to serious and respectable orthodoxies, represented by conventional object relations theory. For now, I will confine myself to saying that I accept that Trickster's discourse may seem like garbage to some readers. Yet his refusal to say definitively that *this* is the only reality (for example, an unjust social and economic system) and *this* is utopian fantasy (for example, reform or revolution) is in itself a profound, political statement.

HERMES AND THE MARKET ECONOMY

Hermes is a Trickster of a different order than the Winnebago Trickster, and we grasp something more specific about politics from his myth. We grasp something about capitalism and the market economy. Hermes is certainly deceitful and criminal, but as we shall see in the myth, the accent is equally on his constructive and transformative nature. After all, Hermes is a god: guide of souls to the underworld, the divinity of olive cultivation, athletics, boundaries, commerce, and messenger of the gods. Hermes stands as a liminal presence, on the threshold or boundary of depth psychology and politics. Hermes also shows that the Trickster and the market economy are somehow connected. The tale of Hermes is, in many ways, the pattern of our particular socio-economic epoch which, like him, is a shape-shifter with numerous names to match its myriad presentations: late capitalism, late-late capitalism, post-capitalism, post-Fordism, the information culture, post-industrialism, post-modernism and so forth.

In the myth, we hear of the deceit and lying of Hermes. This inspires associations to economic inequality, stock market fraud and insider trading. We also hear of the capacity of Hermes to bargain and negotiate. That inspires associations to the potential of liberal democracy to avoid oligarchic hegemony and gross injustice. Let's consider each of these in turn and then try to hold these particular sides of Hermes together in imagination, as a different approach to the splits in the image of the market economy that I referred to in the opening section of the paper. I suggested there that, by overcoming both schizoid tendencies to make an either/or split between positive and negative assessments, and the temptation to reach an uncritical synthesis, we could establish a credible psychological analysis of economic themes that are not usually approached by depth psychologists.

Difficulties with images of the market economy are of central concern in both West and East as both struggle with their confused reactions to the market economy. In the West, we have to face the fact that in spite of growing disgust, we are still caught in a collective love affair with a rotten social order and an unfeeling culture. We made our commitment to this order of things a long time ago, and however much we may know intellectually that it doesn't work for us on the ethical level, and that there is ambivalence, hate and outrage there as well, we can't seem to break our tie to our lover: economic inequality. It is a deep guilt over the undeniable fact of economic inequality that takes us to the cheating heart of capitalism, the partner we refuse to leave, remaining locked in a relationship whose tensions are driving us crazy with alienation.

Perhaps we should now take a closer look at the Hermetic patterns of this dilemma. Myths suggest patterns for more than inner forces; as Joseph Campbell once put it, myths are also 'social dreams' (1989, p. 130). I would add: 'myths are political fantasies'.

In *The Homeric Hymn to Hermes* (Boer, trans. 1979), Hermes leaps up to look for meat on the first day of his life. Pausing only to kill a turtle and fashion a lyre from its shell, he steals fifty head of cattle from the herd of Apollo, his half-brother. Hermes drives the cattle backwards so that their tracks seem to point away from his stables. According to *The Homeric Hymn*, Hermes was the inventor of fire and he roasts two of the animals he has stolen and makes a sacrifice of this meat to the other gods.

Understandably, Apollo is very upset that his cattle have been

taken and quickly works out what must have happened. Charles
Boer's brilliant, modern translation conveys his agitation: 'Listen
kid, / lying in your cradle, / tell me where my cows are, / and
quick! / We're going to fight this out / and it won't be very pretty!'
Hermes is innocence itself – how could a milk-sucking baby do
such a thing and, as he says, after all, 'I was just born yesterday.'
Doesn't fool Apollo, though: 'You trickster, / you sharpie, / the
way you talk / I bet you have broken into a lot of expensive homes
/ in nights past.' In humorous vein, still, Apollo prophesies that
Hermes will come to a bad end. Hermes sticks to his guns and goes
on denying the theft. The two gods present themselves before
Zeus. Apollo accuses, Hermes declares himself not guilty. But, to
Zeus, all is clear and, with a laugh, he orders the two gods to try to
sort out their differences.

We shall be returning to the narrative of *The Homeric Hymn*. Let
us now react psychologically to the story so far and reflect on its
political implications.

The myth amplifies my earlier remarks about our devotion to the
economic realities of capitalism; how we want, really want,
inequality, cheating and injustice. The fact that there is no reference
in the *Hymn* to Hermes actually eating the meat makes me think of
the non-productive nature of the capital markets. They feed no one
directly and yet accumulate wealth invisibly and inequitably.

What is the psychology of economic inequality? Economic
inequality maintains the social structures of desire. Hermes covets
Apollo's cattle even when he should be at the breast. That he does
not eat the meat tells us that the cathexis, the emotional investment,
is in the wanting and the sense of incompleteness. Such a sense of
incompleteness is by no means a wholly negative phenomenon, for
it acts as a spur to constructive activity. However, the nagging and
gnawing in Hermes' spiritual stomach, which our epoch surely can
recognize, are settled only when, by acquisition, by takeover, by
theft, he gets into a relation with another.

Some might argue that tricksterism cannot constitute a type of
relating. But it is clear that Hermes' magical introjection of food is
more than just a phase or passage on the road to 'true' internalization. Economic inequality itself is tied up with a devotion to

primitive magic, amorality and even criminality, all of which belong to the introjective attitude: it's there, I want it, I don't want to ask for it, I'll take it.

Apollo really responds to Hermes and, as we shall see, things deepen between the two brothers. Hermes gets Apollo's attention and this, too, is part of the psychology of economic inequality. Not only stirring up envy, but really being seen, and even mirrored.

The difference displayed by means of economic inequality has something to do with space for symbolization. What I mean is that the wealthier the individual, family, clan, class, nation, the greater the space for symbolization seems to be. One can afford movies, the theatre, opera, eating in restaurants, and even analysis. These are activities which secure and provide the space for symbolization. Of course, this is illusory. I am not saying that the space is always taken advantage of. I am certainly not saying that the well-off lead richer inner lives. But the illusion that they do is hypnotic. In economic inequality there is located a hope for the richness of the symbolic life. We believe this emotionally even though we know intellectually that such richness cannot be bought.

Another factor in economic inequality that makes this condition psychologically attractive to us is the fantasy that the other does not amount to much, particularly if he or she has less money. The poor other does not count, has been eliminated. Hermes does not worry about Apollo's reaction or even think about Apollo at all when he steals the catttle. If one's space for symbolization expands, it can eliminate the other's space for symbolization, and hence can eliminate the other, or seem to. Economic inequality does away with the anxieties of alterity, of having to relate to people who are psychologically other; it encourages fantasies of insulation and isolation. Rich people do not necessarily have rich consciences, and there is sometimes an absence of conscience in those who can afford the rich person's treatment of analysis in a space secured by a well-paid analyst. (This may not be a problem for state-funded psychotherapy or when large-scale insurance schemes are in operation, extending the range of people who can afford analysis.)

We see the link between economic inequality and emotional isolation in the modern legends of Howard Hughes and Paul Getty

– and also in *The Homeric Hymn* when, after the theft, Hermes elects to spend the night alone, kicking dust over his fire and generally covering up. The fantasy plan is of concealing the crime altogether, so that its perpetrator can walk away. In Hermes' case – and here he truly does represent the unconscious motivation of the modern business tycoon – he walks home to his mother. He tells her of his plans to be the most successful capitalist ever: 'I'm capable certainly / to be thief number one.'

So far, we have been looking at one part of the Hermes story. We saw the myth as a psychological patterning of the unjust and inequitable aspects of market economy capitalism. The myth illuminated our investment in such corruption. Yet the rest of the myth brings out that there is another side. For there is more in humanity than a collective love of a rotten social order and an unfeeling culture. There is also in humanity a collective love of a healthy social order and a commitment to a just culture concerned with alterity and the well-being of all its members. *There is absolutely no contradiction.* Both exist side by side at the same time, and in competition with each other. Both sets of human traits are patterned in the Hermes story. I want to state my argument once more: in our age, in both the capitalist West and the once-communist East, it is very hard to clarify confusions about the market economy.

What follows next in the Hermes story may be taken as a metaphor for the kind of economic relationship capitalism supports rather well. The I–Thou aspects of market relations between people are revealed alongside the ruthless aspects, compassion functioning alongside competition.

We return to the narrative of *The Homeric Hymn to Hermes* at the point where Zeus tells Apollo and Hermes to come to terms. Zeus has made it impossible for Hermes to conceal the theft any longer. Apollo, reunited with forty-eight head of cattle, decides to tie Hermes up, perhaps as a prelude to further punishment. To the sun god's amazement, the thongs he has placed round Hermes' ankles suddenly extend to tie up all the cattle! This trick of Hermes' can be compared with Trickster's use of his penis in the Winnebago Cycle of stories. To placate his older brother, Hermes then plays a tune on his lyre. Apollo is quite transfixed by its beauty, which is unlike any music known before. At this point, Apollo relents. He states his intention to make Hermes his protégé. Apollo will be a kind of theatrical agent for Hermes. He will be an impresario granting space for his musical gifts. Apollo promises Hermes the roles of soul-guide and messenger of the gods. But, in the pecking order, Hermes will most certainly be *under* Apollo. Apollo wants the kind of deal Colonel Parker struck with Elvis Presley. The god of capitalism is to be a wage-slave.

Hermes' response to this offer is to come up with a revolutionary countersuggestion: he will give the lyre to Apollo, if Apollo will give him the cattle. Hermes also takes Apollo up on the job of soul-guide and messenger. They make a bargain – the first bargain – and the imaginative implications for the market economy and for liberal democracy are immense. Exchange and mutuality are now highlighted by the myth; enlightened self-interest can benefit both parties. Hermes the cheating Trickster makes a constructive contribution to political thought.

Apollo installs Hermes as 'being in charge of / exchanges among men / on the nourishing earth'. Being no fool, Apollo also makes Hermes swear an oath not to steal anything from him again. Hermes does so and Apollo gives him the caduceus, the famous staff of the messenger. In this transaction, neither god is altered; gods don't change. It was a bargain, not a transformation and it would not have occurred without the earlier cheating, stealing and lying. Apollo remains the oracular god. Hermes remains the liminal god, the Trickster god, moving freely between Olympus and the earth, helping the gods (saving Zeus' life once in a battle with the giants), lubricating the orgy of trade he has set in motion. But, as the *Hymn* soberly reminds us, 'even though he helps a few people, / he cheats an endless number'.

Both sides of our image and evaluation of the market economy have equal existence and equally significant psychologies. As we have seen, to be able to 'hold' two psychologies in mind means something different from striving for a conjunction, synthesis, or balance of them. What is required is a profound emotional acceptance of the ineluctably negative aspects of the market that cannot be done away with or averaged out. They will always exist and flourish alongside and in competition with more positive aspects. We cannot even begin to identify the positives without identifying, working through and coming to terms with the negatives. A synthesis is by no means the only psychological option available to us. For, in a synthesis of our split image of the market economy, the psychological specificity of *either* its cheating *or* its constructive aspects is lost. We cannot dispense with the psychology of theft so as to enhance the psychology of bargaining. There is a psychological coexistence, acceptance of which opens up the possibility of exploring the social and political implications of these sibling economic modes.

It is important not to idealize the bargaining process. Apollo and Hermes do not cease to eye each other cautiously. There are many different styles of bargaining, and bargaining should not be seen as an exclusively 'masculine' phenomenon. Alongside the desire to make a good deal, the bargaining process supports and fosters compassion for the other, without whom there would be no bargaining possible. As Montesquieu put it, 'Wherever the ways of men are gentle, there is commerce, and wherever there is commerce, the ways of men are gentle.' The bargaining process can be exhilarating and fun – and that is an important part of its psychological viability.

A collective psychology that is infused with a mercantile spirit helps a society to avoid tyranny and promotes an active and diverse social life. Competition and bargaining are ways of resolving conflict as well as of generating it. They do not close down options; that is why I stress the emancipatory potential of doing deals.

These comments on the process of bargaining and its political psychology should not obscure the fact that the two bargainers in the myth have very different standpoints and political philosophies. Apollo stands for order, harmony, hierarchy and the unavoidable knowledge of the oracle. Hermes stands for Tricksterism, revolution, panic, and intuitive knowledge. Apollo stands for the deep *status quo*. Hermes stands for its subversion. The political tension between Apollo and Hermes will always be culturally significant.

The image of the two brother-gods bargaining makes me

wonder how much economic equality a culture should aim at. Also, I wonder to what extent a society should demand of its members that they accept responsibility for the economic well-being of others. Depth psychologists rarely address the questions that arise from an inequitable distribution of wealth. Therefore we do not know very much about the depth-psychological implications of seeking a more equitable distribution. Bargaining between 'haves' and 'have-nots' might seem to have only one outcome were it not for the possibility of the apparently weaker uniting together, and maybe even taking extra-constitutional action. The image of bargaining is, therefore, not an unrealistic basis for a rectification of economic injustice.

In *The Wealth of Nations* (1776), Adam Smith explores how it is that competition actually works in favour of the less powerful, provided that competition is permitted to exist. For example, if manufacturers raise their prices too high, a chance is created for one of them to make an increased profit by selling at a lower price. In this way, competition acts as a kind of regulator upon selfishness. Adam Smith's attitude to self-interest was very even-handed. He observed that self-interest was *the* primary economic motivation but, Machiavelli-like, he never said that self-interest was a virtue. He saw competition as a means of transforming a socially destructive aspect of human behaviour into something more useful. In the parable of the talents, the good servant *trades* with the money – he does not merely invest it (Matt. 25: 14–30). This suggests not only the well-known linkage of religion and capitalism, but also an emphasis upon outcome and utility. The market economy is itself a neutral channel via which a certain kind of activity takes place that can subsequently be psychologically evaluated.

As I said earlier, questions of economics should be the focus of a psychological engagement with processes of political change. The problematic of a more equal distribution of wealth has everything to do with the power relations within a culture and hence with its political organization. But political reorganization, in its turn, cannot be cut off from whatever other processes of resacralization might be taking place. Therefore, at this point, it makes sense to try to draw the themes of the paper together.

There is a process of resacralization going on in Western culture, and maybe the same is true of Eastern Europe as well, though the surface signs may be different. Those who seek to link depth psychology with politics should admit that they too are caught up in this process. Resacralization is essentially a secularization of the divine, following the pattern of Bezaleel, master craftsman of the Ark of the Covenant. Disgust with ourselves, and confusion about capitalism and the market economy fuel the urgency of resacralization. Machiavelli addresses these issues in *The Prince*. Here we find that the essence of politics is to know how to be evil when necessary, without anyone thinking you are evil: a trick. That idea led us to the Trickster and his role in processes of political change. Hermes is a special kind of Trickster and I suggested that exploring the Hermes myth helps us with our confusions about capitalism and the market economy. Hermes holds both the inequitable, unjust, cheating side – and the creative, transformative, compassionate side of the market. Hermes is a passageway to a psychological engagement with the political dynamics of the economic system.

ANALYSIS AND POLITICS

It would be a pity and a mistake to restrict the political significance of Hermes to the impersonal, collective level of political and economic theory and organization. There is also a pressing, personal level. By engaging with Hermes, we also have to engage with the warring sides of our Hermes-selves: on the one hand, our fraud, criminality, belief in magic, and love of economic inequality. On the other hand, our capacity for exchange, integrity, relatedness, flexibility, and love of dignity and freedom. This switching of the focus onto the individual, personal level also provides an opportunity to explore some of the issues I raised right at the start of the paper about the relationship of analysis with individuals and small groups to analysis of political and cultural themes.

It seems to me that there would be little point in working on the orientation of depth psychology to the world if its own basic theories and practices remained completely unaltered. I fully support the continuing practice of analysis with individuals and small groups. But are analysts and therapists to change their theory and practice, or not? Have the many analysts who have written on politics and culture been able to change what they think and do? Does a politically aware analyst work differently from one whose perspective is confined to the inner world? In what ways, if any, is my work affected by my ideas about depth psychology? Have the one-quarter of the members of the British Psycho-Analytical Society who have joined the group called Psychoanalysts for the Prevention of Nuclear War changed the way they think about and practise with their patients? Or is it possible to divorce political interest from analytical theory and clinical practice? Maybe some would argue that such a divorce is desirable.

Earlier, I stated that I wanted to work out a model that would enable us to speak of a political drive, of the political development of the individual, of a political level of the psyche, and, as clinicians, to speak of political imagery, or the politics of imagery. I think it helps to approach these themes indirectly and that it is useful to introduce an amplification from another field of intense praxis in which political consciousness deeply affected a worker: Bertolt Brecht's struggle to evolve a theory of theatrical practice that would truly embody his politics.

Brecht's ideology is most acutely expressed not in his extra-theatrical activities, nor in his 'message' – but in his *practice itself*. Of course, Brecht did not invent the idea of drama with a social conscience, but it is mainly to him that we owe the notion of theatre as an arena for social and political debate. Above all, Brecht's goal was to change the status and role of the audience. The paradox is the creation of the active spectator, participating in an argument rather than identifying with a heroic character. In the old theatre the heroic, individual human being was taken for granted, but in Brecht's epic theatre that notion is under the microscope. As his Galileo says, 'unhappy is the country that needs a hero'. For Brecht, the characters in a play are not heroic individuals, frozen in time, but ordinary persons in a social context, engaged in an episodic narrative. They are part, as we would say nowadays, of a larger text.

I expect many would agree that the analytic patient's material cannot remain linked only to his or her personal situation, or to the working through of innate, instinctually-based phantasies. Links have to be made with his or her culture, *its* traditions and history, and to the patient's racial, ethnic, religious and national origins. But how might this be done, and what changes in theory and practice will be necessary?

An individual leads not only his or her own life but also the life of the times. Jung was supposed to have said that 'when you treat the individual, you treat the culture', meaning that persons cannot be seen in isolation from the cultural matrices that played a part in forming them. Acknowledging that there is such a thing as political development makes us build into our apperception of the individual the impact of the political events of his or her life – the political history of the person. These will have contributed, over time, to the state of political development that has been arrived at. We also have to consider the politics an individual has 'inherited' by reason of family, class, ethnic, religious and national background. However, caution is needed when assessing the part played by the cultural background in political development. Analysts need to be careful not to rely on pre-existing generalized conclusions. These are usually based on what is supposed to be empirical evidence about the 'typical' psychology of this or that grouping. But an analyst's concern should be with the experience of difference, not with the defining of difference; each patient has his or her own difference. Each patient may be seen as struggling towards a recognition, expression and celebration of their own difference. But if we do not bear the caveat about predefinition in mind, then a whole set of delusive complementarities comes into play. For example, Jewish psychology will be contrasted with German psychology, black psychology with white psychology, Catholic psychology with Calvinist psychology, homosexual psychology with heterosexual psychology, female psychology with male psychology. This will be done without paying sufficient critical attention to the processes by which terms such as 'Jewish psychology' and the others arise.

The important point is that groupings like these are not

homogeneous. Though members of the group will have some political experiences in common, the exact nature of the impact of such experiences on political development cannot be predicted. Moreover, there are going to be some ways in which everyone is like everyone else, and some ways in which everyone is different – again, it is important not to say in advance which set or combination of conditions will hold.

There is a second possible implication of that gnomic utterance of Jung's – 'when you treat the individual, you treat the culture'. He may be saying that treating an individual indirectly, and maybe inadvertently, provides some therapy for the culture of which that individual is a part. Presumably this is because of the impact the analysed individual will now have on his or her culture, as a sort of 'change agent'. If this is what Jung meant, then I part company with him here. I do believe it is possible in partnership with others, especially social scientists, to treat the culture, to offer therapy to the political and social systems. But I do not believe this can be done in analysis by producing special individuals who will then go out into the world and heal it. Certainly, analysis can help a person achieve a degree of agency on the private and personal level, and this cannot be cut off from the public and political level. But I find it hard to accept that analysands acquire special political powers or prowess, or constitute the vanguard of a politically transformative movement. The idea that those who have become individuated will have a decisive effect on the world scene does seem to have been in Jung's mind, and one can detect the same kind of notion cropping up throughout the evolution of psychoanalysis. The person who, via analysis, conforms to the reality principle, has achieved ego mastery, become genital, or reached the depressive position, is often represented as belonging to an élite that is not susceptible, or is less susceptible, to the group-psychological pressures of the social and political world that they inhabit.

If there is élitism in my way of thinking, then it is not an élitism based on the special properties of clinical analysis to produce more politically developed individuals. My élitism involves a belief that depth psychology itself has something to offer a multi-disciplinary attempt to make an analysis of culture.

To refer to the political development of the individual is to challenge the boundary that is conventionally accepted as existing between public and private, life and reflection, exterior and interior. If we follow the challenge through, then we will have to consider whether psychopathology – usually a discipline confined to the private and interior realms (though often measured by visible behaviour) – does not also refer to the public and political realms. If there is a psychopathology of politics, then it is valid to think in terms of providing a therapy for culture – but without getting too excited at the mere discovery that there *is* psychopathology in the culture.

In many respects, the ground has been prepared for the challenge to the boundary between public and private by what has happened in depth psychology as well as in socio-political movements such as feminism. As far as depth psychology is concerned, our notion of the intrapsychic, internal world includes the part played by relations with other people. At the same time, relations with other people are enriched and expanded by internal processes and images. Internal imagery links people and fosters their relationships. It follows that to divorce work on the apparently internal from work on the apparently interpersonal is false and limiting. Moving this formulation onto the political level, we can regard political processes in terms of psyche speaking, and internal processes in terms of politics. The field of reference is seamless and continuous. Of course, the field is also partial and divided in that differences between these realms will always exist and require acknowledgement rather than being permanently submerged in a cosmic holism.

The unconscious itself may be understood as having origins outside the person, not only of an archaic, phylogenetic kind, but also resulting from the internalization of social institutions and political processes. Language plays a special role in the making of the unconscious – at once direct and indirect. Unconscious perceptions of the world will not find consciousness without language and language will influence what is perceived and how it is perceived. But even language cannot claim permanent primacy, for language is itself affected by social and political institutions and relations.

There is an interplay between language, social and political institutions, and phylogeny. But all lie outside the individual human person and all constitute a kind of contingency for the unconscious.

It follows that any conception of the unconscious or the psyche that omits to refer to social institutions and political processes will be inadequate. The individual develops on the terrain of social and political relations. One consequence of the internalization of political and social factors from the environment is that the individual's innate political imagination may be repressed so that his or her contribution to political process is stunted and distorted. Here, there is an analogy with what internalization of moral prohibitions stemming from parents and society does to drives such as sexuality or aggression. In addition to the stunting and distorting of the drives, internalization of political and social factors influences the development of object relations. For example, the political climate concerning the balance between self-reliance and state provision may influence the duration and quality of the period of dependence enjoyed by a child. The parallel is with the way in which, on the family level, parental psychology and values form a moral climate in which intense relationships acquire a particular moral tone.

The idea of political development has implications for other areas of psychological theorizing. We may come to see aggression as a politically reparative drive, understanding that aggression often incorporates not only intense wishes for relatedness, but equally intense wishes for participation, in a more co-operative or communal mode, in political or social activity. To be authentically aggressive, angry in the belly, and still be able to be part of social and political processes, is a psychological and ethical goal of the highest order. Moreover, the idea of the political development of the individual will influence our ideas about sexuality. I am thinking of the politically destabilizing functions of the polymorphous Trickster (discussed above), and the politically creative functions of the pluralistic father's erotic playback to his children (see Samuels, 1989a, pp. 72–91).

If these various analogies and parallels are valid, then we must extend them to include the possibility that the political drive may vary, as a quantum, from individual to individual. The political formation of the individual is not entirely a by-product of the family and political environment. If there is an inborn quantum of political drive, and this varies from person to person as part of their constitutional personality, then other sources of stunting and distorting of the political drive can be identified. What happens if an individual of high political drive is born into a family and an epoch of low political drive and activity? Or vice versa? I think that situations of this kind are as likely to produce problems in political development as specifics such as child-rearing practices, infantile traumas, maternal or paternal insufficiency, and so forth. After all, it has become clear that there is no clearcut causal link between the events of childhood and the adult personality. What meaningful patterns may be perceived are often the result of a projection backwards in time of present-day worries and problems onto the past – a kind of fictionalized narrative that lends stability to a person's self-perception but certainly not a more definite causal link than that.

If we do not allow the political drive to express itself and the political self to flourish, then we lose one of the most productive avenues for personal growth and individuation. The individual loses out, as do the prospects for transformation and healing of psychopathology within the political system. We may find our private selves in the public sphere; just as we find psychopathology, hitherto thought the province of the individual, on the collective scene. If politics is a drive, then we cannot speak in terms of deciding whether or not to join in; we are involved as part of the human condition.

I would go further, and say that there is an innate desire to change social and political reality. The argument builds up like this: social and political institutions constitute reality. We know that desires can never be fully realized. Therefore, social and political institutions are not constituted by desire. The relation between social and political institutions is likely to be an inimical one. This is expressed in desire's desire to change social and political reality. There is a sting in the tail here for political activists: at times of social and political transformation, desire's desire for change can take the form of opposing and obstructing whatever political activity is going on. Taking 'desire' very loosely that is perhaps why, at times of political and social upheaval, sexual relationships become more urgent than ever, and are often experienced as a contradiction of the call to political action.

Turning now to the clinical practice of analysis itself, I suggest that, like the theatre that Brecht encountered, we are much caught up with heroisms. We see this in Jung's heroic version of mother–infant separation or in Freud's version of father–son rivalry. But heroism is also present in analysis itself, as when the patient is required to 'overcome' something, 'achieve' something, 'sacrifice' something, 'integrate' (that is, take possession of) something, even 'work' through something. The imagery of analysis is all about struggle *within* the patient and I would not say, from my experience, that this is always a wrong conclusion to draw. But the idea of struggle has resonances and relevances that are collective, reflecting the collective's fantasies. Can they be amplified and picked up? Can, for instance, the changing nature of the patient's parental imagery be interpreted on its own political level? Such shifts might involve questions of concern ('parenting') for the environment or other political topics in which the patient is interested. Can we alter our own interpretive thrust, our own heroism, away from 'you the patient', away from 'we the analysing couple', so that the patient's conflicts are more rigorously connected to the world? 'Exvolvement' as well as involvement? As I suggested, we might want to begin to envision the patient as undergoing political development alongside his or her sexual or aggressive development.

Clinically speaking, I think this means that any image can be approached via its cultural and public presence as well as via its individual and private presence. Sometimes, it is the movement and tension between the individual and the cultural perspectives that is important. For instance, a patient dreamed of a beautiful lake with clear, deep water. His soul, he said, and then he associated to the pollution on Italy's Adriatic coast. In this example, the tension between the individual and the cultural associations was prominent, all the more so because the patient was himself Italian and felt personally affected by Adriatic pollution. What, we may ask, is the role of pollution in such a deep soul? Can the soul remain clear while there is pollution on the Adriatic coast? Did the lake, with intimations of mystery and isolation, clash with the popular, extraverted tourism of the Adriatic region? Or was the patient's concern on the social level, with who owned the lake?

We know that images have the capacity to bridge the divide between consciousness and the unconscious. But there is also a continuous movement, within imagery, between the personal/ individual and the collective/cultural levels. It is a transcendent function of a special kind.

With this thought in mind, Brecht's 'alienation effect' and his idea of 'distanciation' can help us here. The analyst might, in some circumstances, completely reverse the poles of what he or she ordinarily does and work also to *distance* the patient from the emotions engendered by the patient's personal situation. In a sense, the patient is not to identify with him or herself as hero, not to be self-empathic, not even to aim for insight or self-understanding. The patient tries to locate what is public about his or her private conflicts, anxieties, relationship problems, and so forth. This would be a radical course to take and implies the *deprivileging and reframing of subjectivity* in analytical ideology.

I cite the patient's dream of the lake as illustrative of the *problem*, showing *why* this work has to be done; rather than as a model *solution*. When discussing these ideas with colleagues, a worry has often been expressed that one might be influencing the patient or – dreaded word – using 'suggestion'. Sometimes I have been accused of wanting to foist my own political prejudices on to the patient. These arguments are advanced as if suggestion were completely out of the question and hence absent from an average, normal, good-enough analysis; and as if topics like sex and aggression never excited an analyst's prejudiced responses – whereas politics does. Of course, there is always a risk of discipleship in the analytical situation as those who have had training analyses will certainly know. And it is not enough simply to *want* to introduce the political dimension into analysis. One has to engage first with political thought and processes. In the terms of this paper, one cannot leap to Brecht and exvolvement *without* travelling alongside

Bezaleel, Machiavelli, Trickster, Hermes, and Adam Smith.

The worries of those who fear political suggestion will pollute analysis are very important and I would not seek to minimize them – for instance, by pointing out that Freud could cope with the idea that suggestion played a part in the talking cure provided the patient was, in fact, disposed to be suggestible. But these worries may have contributed to a tendency among analysts to suppress their interest in political and cultural topics and in how such topics interact with the evolution of the individual personality. *Above all, these worries highlight our lack of a map or model of the typical, healthy-enough political development of the individual.* We have such maps to guide us in the fields of sexuality, aggression and object relations. But are we not by nature political animals, as Aristotle thought? And, as I have been arguing, is not politics a drive, just as sexuality, aggression and the wish to relate are drives? By 'typical' political development, I have not meant to suggest something expressed in the language of the political issues of the day, though they might constitute the raw material for political development. I have been trying to evolve a new psychological perspective on the inner–outer, private–public, personal–political axes that have formed the body of our discussion.

An individual can be said to suffer from repression of the political drive if he or she cannot engage with a political theme that, consciously or unconsciously, is exercising that individual. My clinical experience is that people are already much more engaged politically than they might think they are. Does such engagement have to be active, or would excitement and sympathy be enough? Or, paradoxically, might not good-enough political development mean withdrawal from political engagement for a period of time? There are now several books on 'moral development' (Kohlberg, 1981; Gilligan, 1982), 'spiritual development' (Fowler, 1981), 'religious development' (Kegan, 1982) and, of course, the development of personality is a well-researched field. So the whole approach is in the *Zeitgeist*.

I am trying to make a psychology which operates on a collective level so that even something extrapolated from the individual situation, and even from case histories, would refer to the more collective aspects of the patient's material. Here, I am thinking of the presence of cultural influences in the unconscious or, conversely, the driving power of mythopoeic imagery in relation to cultural and social performance.

One typical feature of depth psychology is its case-by-case approach, exemplified by the case history, nowadays often referred to as the 'case illustration'. Is the case history genre relevant to cultural and social analysis? At the outset, I must say that, for me, the issue is not connected with the truth or objectivity of the case history. For I never doubt that they are, in a sense, fictions, and that apparently radical notion was widely accepted during my training. To critique clinical narratives as if, these days, claims were being made of their incontrovertibility is to tilt at windmills or, at best, to lambast a methodology rejected by all except a few. Feminism has engaged in a similar debate (e.g., Rosler, 1978). A central tenet of feminism is that the personal can be or is political and feminism has certainly had to come to terms with the 'case history' approach.

I conclude this section of the paper by saying that we need to envision a new relationship between the private and the public, the intimate and the crowded, the secret and the open, the vulgar and the numinous. To continue with theatrical imagery, we need a crowd on the stage and a crowd in the audience. On that crowded stage are individuals who offer their most secret truths to individuals within that crowded audience, sharing a collective experience with them.

POLITICS, CULTURE AND OBJECT RELATIONS

Many problems arise when we employ a psychology derived from work with individuals or small groups in order to engage on the collective level with social, cultural and political themes. In this section of the paper, I critique what I feel justified in calling the 'object relations consensus' in terms of its utility as a base for an analysis of politics or culture. Though I shall be discussing object relations, many of the points I am making are relevant for any other psychology of the individual, were it to be employed in cultural analysis.

First of all, I must explain what I mean by the 'object relations consensus'.

Object relations arose in reaction to what some analysts, mainly in Britain, regarded as an excessive dependence by Freud on quasi-biological ways of thinking. In particular, Freud's way of describing instincts seemed to be out-of-date and mechanistic. His model of the mind often used a hydraulic metaphor and this, it was felt, overlooked the emotional quality and feeling-tone of internal processes and experiences. In object relations theory, the person is depicted as a creature who seeks relationships (even, synthesizing this view with Freud's, as a creature whose drive is to relate). Sometimes, relationships are with whole persons, sometimes with parts of persons; sometimes those 'objects' are external to the self, sometimes they are internal, occupying an internal space or world; sometimes objects which are inside are experienced as if they are outside, via projection, and sometimes, via introjection, the reverse is true. Object relations theory is, therefore, a means of introducing the idea of intrapsychic reality to an interpersonal or even relational approach: inner and outer worlds are both given a place.

As object relations theorists continued to depend heavily on Freud's fundamental work, the idea of psychic determinism was by no means jettisoned. This idea holds that later mental events, traits of personality and symptoms are, to a great extent, determined by earlier mental events. In the evolving field of object relations theory, the implication was that the earliest relationships – the earliest object relations – will have a decisive and determining effect upon later relationships. Given that relationships (inner and outer) form much of human psychological experience, it followed that the earliest relationships required the most intense study in recognition of their overwhelming important role. Thus, the relationship of the very small baby to his or her mother or breast, both in external reality and in internal reality, had to become the focus of theoretical endeavour, observation, and clinical practice. (It is interesting to note that Jung had earlier voiced similar objections to Freud's instinctual theory, and went on to develop a form of object relations theory that has been subsequently refined by analytical psychologists; see Samuels, 1989b, pp. 1–21).

There has been a great debate within object relations theory. This has been between object relations theorists, such as Winnicott and Guntrip, and those psychoanalysts who follow Klein. The debate has been about many matters. One notable argument has been over the question of the importance of the quality of environmental provision (by the real mother). It is claimed that Klein did not place enough importance on the real relationships formed in early infancy. The role of the real mother is said to be very sketchily described in her writings. Conversely, Kleinians argue that theorists such as Winnicott have overlooked the vast, innate apparatus of the newborn baby's mind. This colours the infant's experiences of the so-called real mother so that the apparently outer world mother is, in fact (or rather in fantasy/phantasy) an inner world mother.

Another key dispute is over the status of aggression. Klein took up and developed Freud's idea of the death instinct and so, for her, aggression (and destruction) are regarded as primary, innate elements which cannot but affect early and later mental functioning. Winnicott, on the other hand, argued that aggression, while of the greatest importance, is a secondary phenomenon, the result of frustration of the infant by the maternal environment.

In spite of significant differences like those just mentioned, I propose that a consensus has emerged within object relations theory, taking the form of a synthesis of certain ideas of Winnicott's (and others') and of certain ideas of Klein's (and others'). These diverse viewpoints have a great deal in common. What is more, differences of opinion *constitute* and define a field just as they *divide* it. Kleinians and Winnicottians share the same vertices – that is, each side knows to what the other side is referring. So argument is possible. If they did not have much in common, argument of the detailed kind that has taken place would not be possible.

I feel confident in asserting that differences of opinion between Kleinians and non-Kleinians define the field of object relations because I have found the same to be true in other fields, notably post-Jungian analytical psychology (Samuels, 1985). My study of the often vicious arguments between the various schools of post-Jungians reinforced the idea that emotional investment in dispute implies a connection between disputants. In any event, it is worthwhile getting involved in debates within depth psychology because the clash is more illuminating than the contents of one view or other. What often happens in these depth-psychological debates is that each side claims that it already owns and uses the best points of the other side. So Winnicottians claim to recognize the significance of innate features in human psychology and Kleinians claim to recognize the significance for the infant's emotional life of the quality of the real mothering he or she is receiving. There is a drive towards synthesis based on the grandiosity of each side in the argument!

I have made these opening remarks because I do not want to be thought unaware or disrespectful of the professional culture in which I work and in which Kleinians and non-Kleinian object relations theorists are often at odds. However, informed and sympathetic observers of the British psychoanalytic scene have also noted the many similarities between the views of the two groups that I have outlined above (e.g., Grotstein, 1989).

My suggestion is that the object relations consensus has been fashioned out of the very debates within object relations theory that threatened the unity of the theory. Succinctly, the consensus is that there is an interplay between unconscious fantasy and potential, on the one hand, and the good-enough personal, facilitating maternal environment on the other. I can see that, for many, the emergence of this consensus was a liberating experience, seeming to resolve, once and for all, not only previous controversial discussions within psychoanalysis, but also the perennial nature-versus-nurture argument about human psychology. However, the view that human psychology reflects an interplay between innate and environmental factors, though apparently unobjectionable, denies a great deal. The great debate between those who emphasize that the psyche is an autonomous source of the inner life and those who emphasize that persons are culturally contingent creatures has been stilled, for the moment, by the object relations consensus in its explicit espousal of both perspectives.

I want to argue that many of the typical habits of thought of present-day object relations psychoanalysis are not helpful, and may even turn out to be delusive, when we come to address political, cultural and social issues. What follows is an unpacking of the biases and assumptions of the object relations consensus, intended to prompt questions about its role in political and cultural analysis. Inevitably, certain aspects of this critique will open up questions about developmental psychology and analytical technique.

Many applications of object relations theory to social, cultural and political issues require, in the first instance, a problematic dichotomy between what is given or innate, and what is discovered experientially in the environment. Object relations psychoanalysis is then permitted to resolve this dichotomy into an elegant narrative of marriage: between unconscious phantasy and external object, between preconception and outer reality, between infant and mother, between background and foreground, between a deintegrate of the primary self and the corresponding external object. It is hard to see how this kind of theorizing helps on the social scale. If we are attempting an analysis of culture, then what do we consider culture's innate aspects? And what constitutes *culture's* environmental factors? The unavoidable way in which innate and environmental realms are first positioned with regard to a single person, so that the object relations consensus can perform its soldering function, makes it difficult to go beyond the individual perspective to a more collective analysis. Psychoanalytic understanding of the ways nature and nurture interact is useful in understanding how people *relate* to the culture in which they find themselves (even if this is still a markedly individualistic account). But psychoanalysis, framed in the terms of the object relations consensus, is not nearly as useful in an analysis of culture *itself*. The assumption that a good-enough environment is all that the innate potential of an individual requires to flower, and that this is determined within the nuclear family and in the first months of life, is hopelessly passive in the face of problematic social and political structures.

The object relations consensus is biased towards a developmental time-frame. That time-frame is mixed up with a search for whatever seems to be fundamental in the psychology of the individual. This, in turn, leads to a confusion in which the earliest processes, events and relations are regarded as templates for later processes, events and relations. Though no analyst claims that the mother–infant relation is the only important one, because it comes first in time, the mother–infant relation has risen to the top of a hierarchy that has come into being. This has led to the down-playing of other kinds of relations: father, sibling, spouse, partner, companion, employer, servant, rival, opponent, God. I would go further: even the search for psychological fundamentals and found-ations is a flawed project. Does the psyche have to resemble a house, with foundations, upper stories and a roof? Does the psyche have to resemble anything? Or rather, if we want to say that the psyche resembles a house, and that the mother–infant relationship represents the foundations, shouldn't we make room for an ack-nowledgement that this is one of many possible metaphors? *One cannot discount the effect on thought of the raw material of any metaphor employed to facilitate thought* (see Samuels, 1989a, pp. 27–8, 46–7, 56–7, and *passim*).

The idea of development is not to be taken as a 'natural' approach to psychology. 'Development' has its own history and evolution; the idea of personality development is itself subject to contingency. We have to accept that development is an invention and continues to move in the realm of artifice, not to mention fantasy, on the part of developmental theorists. Freud was aware of this. In a remark-able letter to Fliess, written in 1898, he cautions that 'the mirror image of the present is seen in a fantasied past, which then prophetically becomes the present' (Masson, 1985, p. 320). Freud admits that the extent of the artifice means that psychic determin-ism derived from developmental psychology can never be wrong – which may explain its persistence even after 'the death of the psychoanalytical past is a *fait accompli*' (in Frank Kermode's words (1985) in the 1984 Ernest Jones Lecture).

The object relations consensus is biased towards diachrony: changes over time are seen as causal, historical, biographical, temporal, chronological, sequential, successive explanations of phenomena in terms of an unfolding from specific origins. Now, no contemporary depth psychologist can stand outside this tradi-tion; this critique of mine comes from within. But, with cultural and political analysis in mind, I want to question the privileging of the developmental approach. The developmental focus may even be intensifying in depth psychology – I am thinking of psychoanalytically-influenced experimental work on early mother–infant states; and of the systematic observation of infant–mother interaction at home, now a staple in many psychoanalytic and psychotherapeutic trainings.

The object relations consensus is biased toward causality, no matter how subtle this has become. Reference to 'traces' of the real mother, which are found in the transference experience of the analyst-mother, does not go beyond a causal explanation nor significantly revise Freud's original insight into transference (Bollas, 1987, e.g., p. 26). Similarly, spiral models of development, in which elements of personality co-mingle in differing ways at different points of life, are caught up in the same developmental imagery. The spiral is always going *somewhere*, and its development is continuous. Stasis, circularity and discontinuity are overlooked. *Diachrony avoids the integrity of the now.* I am saying that no matter how polished the use of object relations becomes, developmental, diachronic and causal models dominate. Though I am fed up with the constant New Age idealization of a less rational and non-human approach to time, the challenge of such ideas to the time-frame of the individual is relevant here. Why should the time-frame of an individual be relevant for whole societies and cultures?

It may be argued that I have missed the point, that infancy itself is only a metaphor, that 'the baby' is just a means of accessing human nature (baby as everyman or everywoman), that the whole range of primitive processes going on in a baby go on in an adult in just the same way (baby as grown-up), and that society functions in a broadly similar way (baby as social system). Perhaps that is the intention of some theorists – I am not sure; but what has happened is that adults are treated (in both senses of the word) as if they were babies; the metaphor is literalized. What is more, the inevitable regressions which take place in analysis, which analysis fosters, are taken concretely as referring to infancy. Taken more symbolically, which they would be if infancy were indeed being understood metaphorically, such regressions would refer to other things, such as regeneration, psychological deepening, and the additional non-concrete, symbolic aspects of regressive fantasy (see Samuels *et al.*, 1986, pp. 129–30). Moreover, even if infancy is nothing but a metaphor, we still cannot get out of the past–present linkage because, as I mentioned earlier, the raw material (the images) of a metaphor goes on pulsing, suffusing the metaphor on its own raw terms. Claiming that infancy is a metaphor cannot disguise the impact of the literal infant on every aspect of our thinking about psychology that is carried out on the basis of an 'infancy metaphor'. Metaphors stem from the unconscious and, hence, have a powerful life of their own.

The object relations consensus is biased toward complementarity. For example, the image of container/contained has become a concept, referring to what are claimed to be the key characteristics of the mother–infant (or most, or any) relationship. Now, clearly, if two people are in a relationship, one could say that they are contained by the structure of their relationship, or by the typical structure of relationship itself. But that is completely different from seeing it as characteristic of any relationship that one member should 'contain' the other. Is relationship only about containment? Is that what it is *for*? What about exchange, mutuality and equality? Is containment even *the* characteristic of the mother–infant relationship that it is sometimes claimed to be?

In the rise and general acceptance of containment theory, we can see something numinous and fascinating at work: here, the *numinosum* is the image of mother and infant. Jung defined the *numinosum* as a 'dynamic agency' which 'seizes and controls the human subject, who is always rather its victim than its creator' (1940, para. 6). A *numinosum* orchestrates the many variables in a particular situation into one overwhelming message, which can be all to the good, for, without the presence of the *numinosum* in psychological thinking, there would be no sense of discovery. In religious or other powerful experiences, it often happens that the individual is seized by something outside him or herself and that something seems possessed of a fascinating and awe-inspiring power. This is the kind of experience described by Rudolf Otto in *The Idea of the Holy* in 1917 as a numinous experience. But the *numinosum* can also fascinate to the point of tyranny, and ironically, it is the image of mother and infant that object relations theory set out to explicate that now tyrannizes it. The professionals have become fascinated, even hypnotized, by the very images that their professional skills and insights uncovered. This leads directly to the tendency, which becomes unavoidable, to treat society as if it were a baby.

The object relations consensus is biased towards wholeness. I am referring to stress on the way in which part-objects do or do not develop into whole objects. Part-objects get a bad press. Experientially, part-objects are often the source of feelings of wholeness, and in its scanning of part-objects for signs of movement towards whole objects, object relations theory is just as much in the grip of a maturation morality, and is just as normative, as Freud's strictures on love and work, or genitality. Object relations has a problem in its refusal to take the expression in personified form of the multiplicity and plenitude of the psyche as other than a kind of madness or, at best, immaturity. However, part-objects sometimes develop into sub-personalities and perform *as* persons inhabiting the inner world. One can engage in valuable dialogue with these inner persons. What is crucial here is that these Trickster-like states of mind should be valued just as they are, no matter that object constancy is absent. The social and cultural functions of schizoid phenomena, for example in ritual, deserve recognition (see Plaut, 1975). It is not enough to tinker with the order of events in models of development, as some have tried to do, postulating an initial whole object followed by part-objects, followed by whole objects again. The tenor is still unquestioningly developmental, and moralistic. My guess is that, in the next few years, we will see an unravelling of the naturalistic fallacy at the heart of the object relations consensus – that is, the way its 'is' has become an 'ought'.

Alongside the normative thrust of the object relations consensus, there is an overt and a covert claim to universal applicability and validity. But object relations theory cannot be the last word on the human psyche. Object relations arose in particular circumstances and do a particular job: first, in an England frightened as ever of metaphysics (and hence of metapsychology) and, second, to rescue Freud's poetic and humanistic insights from his scientistic aspirations (and those of his translator). The object relations consensus, with its roots in intense ideological conflict within psychoanalysis, has become insulated from these contentious roots and, hence, unable to comprehend its own rhetorical devices and argumentative intents. In the market-place of psychological thinking, the object relations consensus has one stall among many, and by no means is there a special place reserved for it.

I mentioned earlier that there were difficulties with the ways in which object relations psychoanalysis depicts the interaction of individual and culture, and I want to discuss some of them concerning projective identification. The work done on projective identification, whether as early defence, later pathology, or as a means of communication, is something no analyst can ignore. But, as Meltzer noted, there are still questions to be answered about how it 'works', how other people are affected by a person's projections, and how such projections are transmitted. The bias toward projection – a throwing across – suggests an empty space between people across which psychic contents are hurled. But if we challenge the assumption of empty space upon which projective identification depends, and replace it with a kind of ether in which people live, then the javelin is replaced by a woodworm: contents from the one crawl across the as-if-solid ether and burrow into the other. If we take the ethereal image onto a more solid plane and re-image the two people as two stalks of a plant feeding off their single rhizome, then we would have to conclude that *they were never separate people at all*, or at least not to the extent that the idea of projection requires. On the contrary, they were always linked. Whatever we may think about states of union, whether they are illusory or not, their presence has a long history in the theories of depth psychology: as primary narcissism within a person, or as primary mutuality between people. *Perhaps we need to dig out the social and communal implications of these psychological theories that do posit states of non-separateness.* The concept of projective identification just doesn't get hold of the collectivity of persons and, hence, projective identification is a weak tool when it comes to analysis on a collective (social, political, cultural) level.

I would like to give a few instances of the problems caused by the application of the object relations consensus to political, social and cultural analysis. (I gave one example concerning France in 1968 right at the start of the paper.) I am avoiding giving precise references, though all the material has been published in the last three years, so as not to personalize the discussion. Consider the following statements:

> [War] allows people and nations to relapse into the very dubious satisfaction of the state of mind Melanie Klein called the paranoid-schizoid position.

> In controlling inflation, which it undoubtedly has done, the Thatcher administration can therefore be experienced as one which restored governmental authority over the greedy disorder of the British people.

> Our culture suffers from a collective, depressive delusion that it is all-bad, all-destructive.

> Confronted with the real terror of annihilation, our schizoid defences are increased . . . splitting and projection are increased. There is also a regression to part-object relationships, which exclude empathy, compassion and concern.

I want to say right away that, in many respects, I can see the sense in all these statements precisely because I grew up within the traditions of the object relations consensus which underpins them. Nevertheless – even though to say this has also meant self-criticism – these statements reveal the biases of object relations: the biases towards projection, towards universality, towards wholeness, towards causality, and towards diachrony. We see these biases in the use of words like 'regression' or 'relapse', in the harsh attitude to the paranoid-schizoid position (itself a paranoid-schizoid attitude?), in the apperception of Mrs Thatcher as a restorative, containing figure in respect of British, infantile greed. Is greed always a disorder? Striking, as well, is the pervasive presence of 'the baby', the one to whom we are supposed to regress and whose very early styles of functioning we are supposed to replicate when threatened.

The baby is not mentioned directly in some of these examples because the aim was to say something about society. What has happened is that 'baby' and 'society' have become almost interchangeable. The moralizing of the writers is equally significant: when the paranoid-schizoid position is offered as an account of a particular kind of political, social or cultural malaise, what is accepted and uncritically assumed to follow is that the depressive position is the only possible basis for a healthier state – and is even the cure. Therefore, we (society, the world) should get into the depressive position.

To summarize my view: the use of certain models of the mind derived from clinical work with individuals and small groups does not help, and may hinder, attempts to break the psychoanalytic self-proving circle and engage depth psychology and culture. The object relations consensus suffers from a norm-making enmeshment with the numinous and fascinating image of mother and infant, leading to the moralistic advancement of the depressive position as a nostrum for political, social and cultural ills.

ANALYTICAL METHOD AND CULTURAL ANALYSIS

No matter what model of the mind is adhered to, analytical *method* may still be a valid way of approaching political, social and cultural issues – a way of practising cultural analysis. This is true despite the origin of analytical technique in the clinical situation. The cultural analyst strives to get into a transference–countertransference relationship with the cultural problem. Just as in an individual analysis, fostering this relationship means allowing him or herself to be influenced by that which it is hoped to treat or heal: accepting the transference and the experience of countertransference. The countertransference is the place where we find, among other more clinically useful features, the analyst's own unresolved cultural problems and prejudices, evidence of unfinished political development on his or her part. To the degree that he or she can still be rational, the analyst tries to understand the behaviour of the cultural problem in terms of its antecedents. When there is no individual patient, this understanding means finding out the history of whatever problem is under scrutiny, including the myth or myths which attach to the problem. Finally, the cultural analyst tries to raise the level of the culture's consciousness so as to allow the culture to gain a degree of control and knowledge of the problem. This task is accomplished to some extent, and as usual, by interpretation. Social problems, like individual patients or small clinical groups, will respond to 'treatment' in different ways. The hope is to avoid the self-deception of 'objective' analysis; this would be analogous with the inhuman application of the worst kind of high-tech or high-minded medical approach. This tone was often adopted by the Social Darwinists of the second half of the nineteenth century, before a sense of the unconscious was at a cultural analyst's disposal. A similar failure to grasp the unconscious dimension of the 'treatment relationship' mars much, though not all, marxist analysis of culture.

Using the technique and method of individual analysis as a model for cultural analysis makes full use of the analyst's affective involvement, and of the way in which he or she is also touched by the cultural problems he or she is analysing. When I write of the use of the countertransference of the cultural analyst, I do not mean to advocate reliance on an instant and emotional response. I mean, as I have shown elsewhere with regard to individual analysis, that the analyst accepts that his or her experiences embody, reflect or are relevant to aspects of the patient's (or culture's) experience. This relevance is on the basis of their joint immersion in a world of imagery, a shared imaginal world that transcends the boundary of private and public (Samuels, 1989a, pp. 143–74). The analyst's bodily reactions are a crucial part in countertransference and, when it comes to cultural analysis, this is also true. Reactions to the surface of modern life, its sounds, smells, shapes. Reactions to the demands of modern life, its crush, bustle, hassle. Bodily reactions, distilled and worked on by the cultural analyst, join images to form a *via regia* to the heart of the culture and *its* pain.

I want to end this concluding section on analytical method and cultural analysis with a note on doing and saying nothing as a means of practising cultural analysis; a salutary reminder of the limited role depth psychologists can play. Generally speaking, political and cultural analysis, as I envision it, would avoid quiet acceptance of things as they are, or meditative emptiness, or an 'Eastern' way to cure the madness of 'Western' society. But these should not be ruled out. 'Sometimes I sits and thinks and sometimes I just sits', was the rural sage's solution. Drawing on professional experience, an analyst can offer the men and women of action – though the most brilliant of them know it already – a trained sense of timing: when to interpret and when to keep silent. Reflection is itself a psychological contribution to the resacralization of culture.

ACKNOWLEDGEMENTS

I would like to thank the following friends and colleagues for their many helpful suggestions; responsibility for the views expressed is, of course, mine: Michael Adams, John Beebe, Karl Figlio, Paul Gordon, Rosie Parker, Barry Richards, Ann Scott, Sonu Shamdasani, Martin Stanton, Bob Young.

NOTE

1 By 'culture' I mean the assembly, limited in time and space, of the social, material, mental, spiritual, artistic, religious and ritual processes of a sizable community. I use the words 'society' or 'societal' in the following senses: the means by which differences between individuals acquire differences beyond those individuals; relations between the individual and the rest of the community; learned forms of behaviour and communication that excite support and approval or condemnation or punishment; relations between organizations and groups; and as a simple (!) anithesis to 'individual'. The 'collective' implies what is held in common, ranging from a biological/phylogenetic sense of collective, to something like the collective atmosphere in a crowded theatre or football stadium.

REFERENCES

Ali, T. and Brenton, H. (1990) *Moscow Gold*. London: Hern.

Beebe, J. (1981) 'The Trickster in the arts', *San Francisco Jung Institute Library Review* 2: 95–110.

—— (1984) 'The father's anima', in A. Samuels, ed. *The Father: Contemporary Jungian Perspectives*. London: Free Association Books, 1985/New York: New York University Press, 1986, pp. 95–110.

Boer, C. (trans.) (1979) *The Homeric Hymn to Hermes*. Dallas, TX: Spring.

Bollas, C. (1987) *The Shadow of the Object: Psychoanalysis of the Unthought Known*.

London: Free Association Books.

Campbell, J. (1989) *This Business of the Gods*. Caledon East, Ontario: Windrose.

Fowler, J. (1981) *Stages of Faith*. San Francisco, CA: Harper & Row.

Gilligan, C. (1982) *In a Different Voice: Psychological Theory and Women's Development*. Cambridge, MA: Harvard University Press.

Grotstein, J. (1989) 'An American view of the British psychoanalytic experience: psychoanalysis in counterpoint'. Unpublished.

Jung, C.G. (1940) *Psychology and Religion, Collected Works*, vol. 11. London: Routledge & Kegan Paul/Princeton, NJ: Princeton University Press.

Kegan, P. (1982) *The Evolving Self*. Cambridge, MA and London: Harvard University Press.

Kermode, F. (1985) 'Freud and interpretation', *Int. Rev. Psycho-Anal.* 12:3–12.

Kohlberg, L. (1981) *The Philosophy of Moral Development*. San Francisco: Harper & Row.

Kohut, H. (1971) *The Analysis of the Self*. New York: International Univ. Press.

—— (1977) *The Restoration of the Self*. New York: International Universities Press.

Machiavelli, N. (1514) *The Prince*, G. Bull, trans. Harmondsworth: Penguin, 1961.

Masson, J. (1985) *The Complete Letters of Sigmund Freud to Wilhelm Fliess 1887–1904*. Cambridge, MA and London: Harvard University Press.

Otto, R. (1917) *The Idea of the Holy*, J. Harvey, trans. Oxford and London: Oxford University Press, 1923.

Phillips, K. (1990) *The Politics of Rich and Poor*. New York: Random House.

Plaut, A. (1975) 'Object constancy or constant object?', in A. Samuels, ed. *Psychopathology: Contemporary Jungian Perspectives*. London: Karnac Books, 1989. New York: Guilford Publications, 1991.

Radin, P. (1956) *The Trickster: A Study in American Indian Mythology*. New York: Schocken, 1972.

Rosler, M. (1978) 'Is the personal political?', in R. Parker and G. Pollock, eds *Framing Feminism: Art and the Women's Movement 1970–1985*. London and New York: Pandora, 1987, pp. 146–60.

Samuels, A. (1985) *Jung and the Post-Jungians*. London and Boston, MA: Routledge & Kegan Paul.

—— (1989a) *The Plural Psyche: Personality, Morality and the Father*. London and New York: Routledge.

—— (ed.) (1989b) 'Introduction' to *Psychopathology: Contemporary Jungian Perspectives*. London: Karnac Books. New York: Guilford Publications, 1991.

—— (1993) *The Political Psyche*. London and New York: Routledge, forthcoming.

Samuels, A., Shorter, B. and Plaut, A. (1986) *A Critical Dictionary of Jungian Analysis*. London and New York: Routledge & Kegan Paul.

Smith, A. (1776) *An Enquiry into the Nature and Causes of the Wealth of Nations*, ed. E. Cannan. New York: Modern Library, 1937.

Young, R. (1991) 'Psychoanalytic critique of productivism', *Free Assns* 2: 507–14.

Address for correspondence: 17 Archibald Road, London N7 0AN, UK

Commentaries on 'The mirror and the hammer'

1. Karl Figlio

During a symposium on countertransference, Donald Winnicott said to Michael Fordham:

> Incidentally, may I remind Dr Fordham that some of the terms he uses are not of any value to me because they belong to the jargon of Jungian conversation. He in turn can tell me which of my words are useless to him. I refer to: transpersonal, transpersonal unconscious, transpersonal analytic ideal, archetypal, the contra-sexual components of the psyche, the animus and anima, animus–anima conjunction.

> I cannot be communicated with in this language. For some in this hall these are household words, and for the rest they have no precise meaning (Winnicott, 1960, p. 159)

A few years later, Winnicott said:

> In our theory it is necessary to allow for both a male and a female element in boys and men and girls and women . . . These considerations have involved me then in a curious statement about the pure male and the pure female aspects of the infant boy or girl (Winnicott, 1966, pp. 93, 96)

Free Associations (1993) Volume 3, Part 4 (No. 28): 594–603

I do not know whether Winnicott's encounters with Fordham primed him, perhaps unconsciously, for his recognition of contrasexual components of the psyche, which are integral to Jungian theory and which, otherwise, might have had 'no precise meaning'. It is also possible that he was drawing the sting from kneejerk, anti-Jungian sentiment among psychoanalysts, given that he and Fordham were quite familiar with each other's ideas, having engaged in regular discussion over many years through the Medical Section of the British Psychological Society (including the symposium on countertransference in 1959, which produced several classic papers on the subject and from which the quotation above is taken).

The juxtaposition of Winnicott's apparent unwillingness to be spoken to in a foreign language with the richness of his thinking, including his capacity to assimilate 'foreign languages', gives us a standard by which to assess responses to Andrew Samuels' interjection into the psychoanalytical understanding of cultural processes. In referring to this incident, I hope similarly to draw the sting from any hasty objection to unfamiliar images and concepts, and to invite readers to share my appreciation of his fertile thinking.

Samuels wants to force the reader into foreign territory and into listening to a foreign language. Indeed, he argues that the growth points in a field occur where there is a disruption to understanding, not where there is a disagreement: debate holds together a consensus through mutual projections; but the disruption of intelligibility – when one cannot understand what the other is saying, and vice versa – are replete with potential. That's why he traces out the Kleinian/Winnicottian debate over innate destructiveness and environmental provision: he wants to show that it sustains an object relations consensus that blocks a view of culture as an autonomous realm with innate, psyche-like properties.

For Samuels, psychoanalysis cannot plumb culture to a great depth because the object relations consensus has a restricted view of its properties, limited to those of the environment that nurture the psyche. The psyche develops historically, in a diachronic frame in which later events build on earlier events in a linear causal sequence. With culture as its nurturing environment, collective life is only the sum of individual lives in that cultural medium.

But if culture has innate properties – like psyche – then, as cultural analysts, we can respond to it, as to another person: we can have a countertransference to it. Countertransference to culture is foreign territory, and the implications of Samuels' language are explicit and disturbing. The reader might want to say, 'When Samuels speaks of a countertransference to culture, the terms he uses are of no value to me. I cannot be communicated with in this language.'

Samuels means what he says. Otherwise, how would his cultural analysis differ from political commentary, from journalism, from history-writing? How would the analyst's responses differ either from the political or cultural analyst's cognitive responses, based on his or her theoretical background and research; or from the ordinary observer's emotional responses?

By putting the emphasis on countertransference, Samuels distinguishes his cultural analysis from other cultural studies, such as the long tradition of participant observation in sociology, which produced the classic studies of the 'Chicago School' (though it must be noted that the concept and the name were formulated by Harry Stack Sullivan, a major figure in psychoanalysis in the United States; see Figlio, 1987).

Samuels implies that there is something particular about the receptive, tuned and disciplined responses of the cultural depth psychologist, parallel to countertransference in the consulting room. We have to draw an additional implication from Samuels' thesis, as well: one that will make it still more disturbing. In speaking of countertransference, Samuels implies that culture has a transference to the analyst – that they are caught up in a relationship. It has to be so, not just because countertransference has meaning only with respect to transference, but because the effect of the cultural analyst on culture must be understood in the same terms as the culture's effect on the analyst. If Samuels believes that cultural analysis has an impact – that culture listens to the analyst – then our understanding of that effect must be couched in the same analytic language.

For Samuels, as for Jung, the therapeutic relationship enmeshes both patient and therapist through the unconscious dimension of their relationship, disturbing the therapist and requiring transformation in both parties. Samuels argues that the cultural analyst, like the individual analyst, allows him or herself to become influenced by the analysand. The cultural analyst will experience unresolved prejudice just as the individual analyst will experience unresolved psychopathy, and the same sort of unconscious enmeshment will bind the cultural analyst to his or her culture. Not only will this entanglement push to the surface 'evidence of unfinished political development on his or her part'; but also his or her discipline and familiarity with these processes will, as in the case of individual analysis, incline the analyst to accept 'that his or her experiences embody, reflect or are relevant to aspects of the patient's (or culture's) experience . . . on the basis of [a] shared imaginal world that transcends the boundary of private and public' (p. 591).

Despite these strictures, cultural analysis might, at first, sound arrogant, as if the analyst were standing apart from events and pronouncing upon them. But it's not: it refers to an analytical frame that is consistent with established clinical and theoretical principles. It reminds me of Jung's interpretation of the Papal Bull of Pius XII, *Munificentissimus Deus* (1950), which promulgated the Assumption of Mary (Jung, 1954, ch. 19). This event, open to ordinary historical documentation by scholars, was interpreted by Jung as the bringing together of feminine and masculine principles; as the culmination of a cultural urge over decades; as if the Papal Bull were 'needed', in its symbolism, to resolve a centuries-old irregularity. I am also reminded of Jung's book on flying saucers (1959), which he saw as mandala projections into the dark night sky: culturally 'needed' symbols of wholeness in periods of upheaval. I mention these two documents to indicate that, for a substantial body of analytic practitioners, events are cultural symbols – unconscious attempts to bring a resolution between incommensurable positions – apart from the personal meanings that may be ascribed to them. They are not empty, waiting to be invested with individual projections: they are redolent with meaning as collective immanences.

It is a mode of thinking foreign to many psychoanalysts; yet they operate freely with concepts such as projective identification and containment, which are unrelated to any known biological or physical principles. Indeed, Samuels restricts the field to a definable range of phenomena by imposing countertransference (and transference is logically entailed) as a parameter of enquiry: just as the countertransference phenomena in the clinical setting have to be demonstrated, not assumed, so too does he imply that the equivalent material of cultural analysis will have to be demonstrated and tested. Perhaps the unconscious of cultural analysts will need monitoring in a supervisory relationship. The evolution of methodology will produce research techniques, literature, training and monitoring.

The other implication of cultural countertransference has already been mentioned: the cultural analyst will be enmeshed in transference pressures of the culture. Such a relationship should discourage interpretive pronouncements that, for example, refer to paranoid-schizoid aspects of events, and thereby maintain a distance between the analyst and the object of interpretation.

Samuels is proposing a depth psychology appropriate to collective life, a radical proposition that entails a new dimension. In such an endeavour, it is easy to slip from the rigours of winning and fortifying a new territory; and I think Samuels does slip. In his example of the patient who dreamed of the beautiful, clear, deep lake, associated with his soul, then with pollution, Samuels moves us from the possibility that his patient is thinking of his soul and of its remaining clear when surrounded by pollution, over to the socio-economic situation of the Adriatic region (pp. 576–7). It seems to me that, at this point, at least three different themes come to the fore: first, the objectification of the social situation, which refers to the patient's political maturity; second, the technical decision, as to whether to treat material transferentially (and, therefore, countertransferentially) or to allow – indeed to promote – a reflectiveness in another dimension; third, the ethical decision, as to whether the analyst's motives and prejudices are well enough monitored and controlled. The slippage occurs between these three aspects of the clinical situation, and in the models Samuels chooses to keep the reader's mind inside the new territory he wants to explore.

The technical and ethical issues do not amount to anything. Samuels has argued for a cultural countertransference equivalent to an individual countertransference, which brings problems that trouble him, such as suggestion, under the rubric of theoretical understanding, monitoring and control: cultural countertransference is not the same as a personal reaction to the cultural imagery evoked in both therapist and patient, just as the countertransference is not the same as a personal reaction to the patient. But to the extent that the literature and practices concerning countertransference denote an objective situation, suggestion and prejudice are as irrelevant theoretically as the misreading of an instrument is irrelevant to the theory that underlies a particular experimental measurement. An improper intervention – whether it be, on the surface, about the clinical setting or about the Adriatic region – is one that gratifies the patient's needs in a direct way and, in doing so, interferes with the reflectiveness that is consistent with depth psychology. Samuels' own views on ownership and pollution in the Adriatic are, therefore, relevant neither to the patient's transferential nor to his political maturity.

Although depth psychologists have not characterized political maturity, they would no doubt seek consistency with psychoanalytic notions of psychological maturity. They might include the quality of object relations such as objectivity in perception, and a relative freedom from compulsive dependence and gratification of infantile needs through control of one's objects. On that assumption, the technical and ethical situation for both cases is well described by Michael Balint;

> If we accept these ideas [which characterize a non-omnipotent relationship], then the problem of whether or not to gratify a regressed patient's cravings appears in a different light, so different that doubt arises whether we have not been struggling with a false problem which can never be solved because it is wrongly formulated. The real problem is not about gratifying or frustrating the regressed patient but about how the analyst's response to the regression will influence the patient–analyst

relationship and by it the further course of treatment. (Balint, 1968, p. 168)

As to the 'distanciation', 'alienation effect' and objectification of the social situation, and its implied 'deprivileging and reframing of subjectivity', we will have to see: here is a new research area, which we can't know about in advance. What we must do is retain a conceptual precision, so that we can distinguish technical and ethical decisions we already know about from exploration within a new dimension.

Samuels foreshadows this new dimension; indeed the bulk of his paper is an attempt to sketch it in the languages we have available, including myths. From Zeus' refusal to intervene in a conflict between Apollo and Hermes, we learn that the resolution of psychic conflict must be sought in the coexistence and complementarity of psychic forces, not in the paranoid phantasy of exterminating whatever is unwanted by a dominant personality. From the Trickster, we learn that transformative possibilities arise in uncanny ways. From the detailed instructions on building the Ark, we learn that the sacred has always existed in everyday life. Noah's Ark, the Ark of the Covenant, the archive in which we keep records of human history and the archaeology through which we reconstruct the everyday life of our ancestors span the divine and human worlds.

One problem for the psyche in striving to live too closely with the divine is what Jung called inflation, in which one tries to bring fundamental psychic and social processes within the sphere of individual mastery (the self identified with an archetype): hubris, omnipotence, arrogance, grandiosity, narcissism all convey something of this danger.

Myths may communicate immediately an archaic unconscious dimension, but they need to be integrated into consciousness through slow, careful scholarship. That requires reductive analysis, the association of myth with historical situation (as Samuels himself argues), the study of comparative myth, the evolution of language, the (psycho)logical entailment of consequences within myth – the overall, rational interrogation of myth.

In my view, Samuels criticizes reductionism incorrectly, and sets up a false opposition between it and a depth psychology in which all phenomena, whether apparently inside or outside a self, are understood as psyche-like; in which material reality is sacred. I will call this view 'psychoid', in line with Jung's language for a psyche-like aspect of phenomena, as opposed to their natural-causal aspect. For example, Samuels sees the psychoanalytic conceptualization of splitting in terms of a regressive avoidance of whole-object relations in the depressive position, which he contrasts with the psychoid view of splitting as the basis on which sub-personalities – which carry aspects of the personality unavailable to, and perhaps unwanted by, the dominant personality – can develop.

I think his mistake is to see these concepts as ontological rather than epistemological: he identifies splitting with part-objects as entities, rather than treating it as a process aimed at omnipotent control over a world sensed as external to the self. The breast as a part-object is not an anatomical structure, but a phantasy of the source of sustenance and of threat. Its nature drives from the libidinal orientation of the ego to its object (e.g., oral) and from the latter's threatened autonomy from the ego.

From this confusion of ontological and epistemological understanding of splitting, Samuels establishes the ontological existence and contribution of sub-personalities, as well as the advantage of a psychology that gives a place for these psychic institutions that have been excluded by psychoanalysis. His new depth psychology builds, in part, on an opposition between it and psychoanalysis. I can see what he is getting at, in that the analysis of the psyche in terms of defence implies an emphasis upon the distortion and inhibition of psychic development; and it may be that the confusion I have attributed to him could equally be laid at the door of psychoanalysis.

In my view, reductionism is simply the precise connecting of premisses with conclusions – the working out of logical entailment. In an empirical frame, reductionism means that one assumes a similar kind of entailment, whether or not one eschews any notion of a deep structure of reality, according to which things happen 'logically'. To use the example of splitting again: splitting is, from the standpoint of anxiety and defence, an avoidance of loss and guilt (regression from the depressive position); from the standpoint of fragmentation it entails idealization and forming dependable object relations; from another standpoint, it will mean something else. The problem only arises when one tries to reify split-off objects.

Samuels weakens his case by his criticism of reductionism, but he weakens it in another, more surprising, way. When he suggests a model for collective life more appropriate to the innate character of culture than the individualistic concept of projective identification, Samuels draws upon the physical notion of an ether and upon a biological structure, the rhizome of a plant. What stands out about these two models of the collective essence of individuals – how they share in a common cultural life – is that they are concrete and picturable. The 'joint immersion in . . . a shared imaginal world', the 'social and communal implications of these psychological theories' that 'perhaps we need to dig out', are a kind of tuber or an underground part of a plant, shared in common by roots and leaves; or, more abstractly, a rarefied, ethereal substance postulated to explain unseen connections between objects.

Why does he backtrack? Why does he plant a bold hypothesis in inappropriate, depleted soil that cannot nourish it? Leaving aside the concrete biological imagery, it's as if the counterintuitive worlds of quantum and relativity physics did not exist. Samuels becomes curiously reductionistic, not in the sense of conceptual precision in drawing consequences from premises and models, but in the reified sense of limiting thought to restrictive, concrete models.

I will close with a personal preference. Samuels has proposed a notion of culture as psyche, and he has strictly drawn consequences from it: that an analytic relationship is imaginable and that it would be characterized by a countertransference relationship (I would add transference as well). If that is the case, then there is a literature, a methodology and a practice that becomes immediately relevant. If his proposal is counterintuitive, it is no more so than the proposition in quantum physics that a particle can move from one place to another without passing through the space between; nor than the proposition in geometry that the shortest distance between two points needn't be the straight line connecting them; nor than the proposition in relativity physics that time-frames vary with speed.

Each of these propositions has redirected the history of human thought and, in turn, has been assimilated to it. Let us draw the reductive consequences from the model and proceed with the research: it is both startlingly new and assimilable to methodical enquiry.

REFERENCES

Balint, M. (1968) *The Basic Fault: Therapeutic Aspects of Regression*. London: Tavistock.

Figlio, K. (1987) 'The lost subject of medical sociology', in G. Scambler, ed. *Sociological Theory and Medical Sociology*. London: Tavistock, pp. 77–109.

Jung, C.G. (1954) *Answer to Job*. London: Routledge & Kegan Paul; Sir Herbert Read, Michael Fordham, Gerhard Adler and William McGuire, eds, *The Collected Works of C.G. Jung*. 20 vols. London: Routledge & Kegan Paul; Princeton, NJ: Princeton University Press, vol. 11, pp. 355–470.

—— (1959) *Flying Saucers: A Modern Myth of Things Seen in the Sky*. Collected Works, vol. 10, pp. 307–433.

Winnicott, D.W. (1960) 'Counter-transference', *The Maturational Processes and the Facilitating Environment*. London: Hogarth and the Institute of Psycho-Analysis, 1979, pp. 158–65.

—— (1966) 'The split-off male and female elements to be found in men and women', *Playing and Reality*. London: Tavistock, 1971. Harmondsworth: Penguin, 1974, pp. 84–100.

Address for correspondence: 24 Rosebery Avenue, Colchester, Essex CO1 2UJ, UK

2. Sonu Shamdasani

Having debated with Andrew Samuels his project for the political engagement of depth psychology under its various tricksterish changes of shapes, I will in the following remarks simply focus on what seem to be certain difficulties in its current articulation. One can applaud Samuels' reiteration of the urgency and the necessity for a psychological engagement with politics; and the way in which his attempt to formulate possible tactics, through shifting the language away from the narrow sectarianism of various analytic schools, sets the stage for the debate (given the current state of their interpolitical relations, this is a significant enough achievement in itself). The critical sections which deal with the pitfalls of various approaches are salutory; in particular, the critique of 'the object relations consensus' and its applications to politics is both timely and important. However, the problematics at issue in having 'the baby' as the paradigm of psychological intelligibility are not resolved through replacing the baby with a set of alternative figurae – in this case, drawn from myth – but require a questioning of the politics of paradigmicity itself. It is here, it seems to me, that the main difficulty of the paper lies, and this concerns what Samuels terms the resacralization of culture, and the way in which he inscribes the psychology of the political within this global paradigm.

Samuels writes: 'My suggestion is that amidst the tragic anomie and baffling atomization; amidst the dreadful conformism of "international" architecture, telecommunications and cuisine; amidst the sense of oppression and fear of a horrific future, an equally fragmented, fractured and complex attempt at a resacralization of the culture is going on. There are many surface signs of resacralization, New Age or New Times thought, expressing concern for the quality of life: green politics, feminism, the human potential movement, finding God in the new physics' (p. 548). He adds born-again Christians and other fundamentalists to this list, and proposes that this is a way of describing what has been happening in Eastern Europe and the former Soviet Union. Samuels sees resacralization as 'a contemporary attempt to shift a sense of holiness into the secular and material world'. He justifies the retrospective temporal sense by speaking of resacralization as connoting 'a feeling level that we sense once existed but we find has vanished from the modern world . . .' (p. 548). He further argues that those who seek to link depth psychology with politics should admit that they too are caught up in this process. Resacralization is essentially a secularization of the divine, following the pattern of Bezaleel, master craftsman of the Ark of the Covenant. Disgust with ourselves, and the confusion about capitalism and the market economy, fuel the urgency of resacralization. He writes that Bezaleel '. . . is the collective image and cultural personification of resacralization, the contemporary drive to render the secular holy' (p. 549).

Samuels describes his analysis of resacralization as 'description, chronicle and interpretation, not sermon or advocacy'. Thus the analysis of resacralization is itself given as an example of the psychologizing of the political being proposed. This analysis is concretely developed in a mytho-political hermeneutics of morality through the Winnebago Trickster myth, and of the market economy through *The Homeric Hymn to Hermes*.

While the banner of resacralization informs the rhetoric and self-description of some of the groups which Samuels lists, needless to say it extends to many who would find themselves radically opposed to such a designation – including many who 'seek to link depth psychology with politics'. The global description of resacralization, no less than the 'object relations consensus', politically enacts a hegemonic operation; while the key question of what legitimates such a depth hermeneutic is not sufficiently raised.

For Samuels, resacralization forms nothing less than a key to an understanding of contemporary history. However, the inclusion of the move to link depth psychology and politics as a further surface expression of this phenomenon seems to beg precisely the pressing and troubling questions which are at stake in the contemporary co-implication of religion and politics, through the occupation of a pregiven territory. For these to be approached, the complex history of the interrelation of religion and politics, of mythic hermeneutics, and of the role of psychology in all this needs to be analysed.[1] (It is greatly to Samuels' credit that he has elsewhere undertaken an excavation of one chapter in this history – namely, how Jung's project of resacralization led to such abysmal results in its encounter with National Socialism (Samuels, 1992)). But would this not call for a suspension, and calling into question, of part of the basis upon which Samuels' call for political engagement currently rests?

To develop a psychology of the political that would give a 'model of the typical healthy-enough political development of the individual' seems to rest on a prior division of this from any determinate politics, or what Samuels terms 'the political issues of the day'. However, as indicated above, this separation is itself underwritten by a contestable claim to understand the current historical predicament in terms of resacralization. Regardless of whether one assents to this depiction, it inscribes the psychology of the political being developed here into a predetermined reading of the current political situation. This then breaches the separation of the psychology of the political and a determinate politics, on which Samuels' affirmation of the possibility of the former rests. Thus the necessity for political engagement, which runs throughout the paper, threatens to undermine its current strategic deployment.

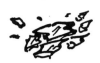

1   I refer here to Claude Lefort's (1988) analysis of the historical bifurcation, on one

side, and drawing together, on the other, of religion and politics; and, on the relation between psychoanalysis and politics, to Philippe Lacoue-Labarthe and Jean-Luc Nancy's 'La Panique politique' and Mikkel Borch-Jacobsen's analyses in *The Freudian Subject* (1988) and *The Emotional Tie* (forthcoming), which are the best to date; and to Mark C. Taylor's deconstruction of the 'sacred and the profane' (1987).

REFERENCES

Borch-Jacobsen, Mikkel (1988) *The Freudian Subject*. Stanford, CA: Stanford University Press.
—— (forthcoming) *The Emotional Tie*. Stanford, CA: Stanford University Press.
Lacoue-Labarthe, P. and Nancy, J.-L. (1979) 'La panique politique', in *Cahiers Confrontation*, no. 2.
Lefort, Claude (1988) 'The permanence of the theologico-political?', *Democracy and Political Theory*. Oxford: Polity Press, pp. 213–55.
Samuels, A. (1992) 'National psychology, national socialism, and analytical psychology', *Journal of Analytical Psychology* 37 (Parts 1, 2): 3–28, 127–48.
Taylor, Mark C. (1987) *Erring: A Postmodern A/theology*. Chicago, IL: University of Chicago Press.

Address for correspondence: 34 Morpeth Mansions, Morpeth Terrace, London SW1 1ET, UK

3. David Mayers

The background from which I approach Samuels' paper is the Kleinian tradition within psychoanalysis; and the Left Opposition to Stalinism within socialism. I say this both to provide a context for my comments; and to lay the ground for a question as to the nature of the debate, which I shall raise later.

Fundamental to psychoanalytic understanding of the individual psyche and the marxist understanding of social process is the distinction between base and superstructure: a distinction which is wholly absent from Samuels' paper. We are the sort of creatures that we are, think as we do, because we have a certain sort of body – Freud stresses that the primitive ego is a bodily ego. We have the society that we do because of the problems of production, exchange, distribution and consumption of material goods; and the struggles between classes to control these processes. Psychoanalysis has given us the concept of rationalization, marxism that of ideology to understand how we try to fool ourselves into believing that things which are given are a matter of choice.

Samuels' wish to deny this distinction, embodied in his use of 'the Trickster', leads him, in line with a body of contemporary thought often called post-modernist, to misrepresent psychoanalysis and to lack the tools for understanding social transformations. At the heart of it is his claim that container/contained or baby/mother's breast are only metaphors for describing the genesis of object-relating. Now there are two points here: first, to describe a way of seeing as metaphorical is to suggest that there are other, equally valid, metaphors which give alternative accounts of our experience. I suggest that psychoanalysis, in isolating certain

Free Associations (1993) Volume 3, Part 4 (No. 28): 608–11

features of infantile experience, has shown that the baby/breast relationship is a fundamental condition for human experience – it is not a matter of judgement but of a structuring condition which makes judgement possible (Wittgenstein is an invaluable source of insight into this sort of distinction). Second, Samuels' appeal to metaphor – describing something in terms of something else – presupposes the possibility of a univocal description without transferential reference: yet this leads him to a privileged description whose existence he originally wished to deny. This is an inherent internal contradiction which vitiates the post-modernist programme.

On the political front, Samuels seems to see capitalism as a form of society which we – or some of us – have voluntarily chosen: rather than as one which rose as a solution to the problems of feudalism's no longer being workable. He argues, again via his Trickster, for the psychological benefits of competitive economic struggle: as though every worker had a capitalist's bank balance in his lunch box; and forgets that the internal logic of capitalism demands that the vast majority of people shall be exploited as producers of surplus value which only their rulers enjoy. Even if we stick, for the moment, to psychological satisfaction, is it really credible that the satisfaction gained by the Ford director or shareholder is the same as that of the worker on the Ford assembly line?

(Samuels' unawareness of class, his naïvely optimistic voluntarism, remind me of Marx's saying that when the petit bourgeoisie, as a class, enters the political arena, it leaves it as untouched and innocent as it went in – Gandhi's India, de Valera's Ireland, Thatcher's Britain.)

The lines on psychoanalysis and politics come together in the claim that culture affects the unconscious. Now this is not a tenable claim within psychoanalysis: or, to put it better, the notion of the unconscious being appealed to here is different from the psychoanalytic one. Whatever analytic tendency we belong to, psychoanalysts regard unconscious material as that which is internal to the individual: culture is a preconscious or conscious derivative. This is not to say that there is no commerce between the internal and external worlds. But it is important to see which way the dynamic goes: psychoanalytically, culture does not influence the unconscious; rather, we borrow from cultural forms and institutions to give expression to our internal life. (For instance: certain forms of persecutory anxiety will find expression in dreams about repressive institutions – schools, prisons, the army, etc.) The internal remains, ontologically, prior. This is not, of course, to show that Samuels is wrong: but to argue that in his Trickster-driven wish to see a continuum between unconscious phantasy and culture, he is radically departing from the psychoanalytic tradition.

This brings me to my final question: what sort of difference is it between Samuels' position and mine – that between colleagues engaged in the same work but holding different points of view, or that between workers committed to fundamentally different programmes? Granted that he has been a prolific and eloquent writer in the Jungian world, I wonder if a central feature of Samuels' analysis is an appeal to Jung's notion of collective unconscious: which seems to me, again, to deny the gap between unconscious phantasy and culture which psychoanalysis posits. This thought makes me suspect that our aims are radically different in this way: that my seeing change towards comparatively depressive functioning at the individual level, and socialism at the political-economic, will seem to Samuels restrictive and lacking in dimension; and his celebration of Hermetic shape-shifting will seem to me reactionary and perverse.

Roger Money-Kyrle listed as the aims of psychoanalysis: seeing the breast as the supremely beautiful object; seeing parental intercourse as the supremely creative act; and accepting the inevitability of death (1971, p. 442). This seems a good starting point for both therapists and socialists: but it has an inherent appeal to a set of values. It says, especially, that hope is better than despair. I wonder if Samuels' theory, as presented in his paper, would allow him to agree with this.

REFERENCES

Money-Kyrle, R. (1971) 'The aim of psycho-analysis', in Donald Meltzer, ed. *Collected Papers of Roger Money-Kyrle*. Strath Tay: Clunie Press, 1978, pp. 442–9.

Address for correspondence: 74 Eton Place, Eton College Road, London NW3 2DS, UK

4. Renos Papadopoulos

In 'The mirror and the hammer' Andrew Samuels attempts to develop a form of cultural analysis based on depth psychology; he endeavours to fashion an approach which would be able to address both the individual and cultural realms with the same strength of relevance. Using Mayakovsky's imagery, it could be said that Samuels seems to avoid the trap of proposing depth psychology either as a *mirror* of society or as a *hammer* with which to shape society. Instead, I would venture to say that his own approach amounts to suggesting a third image, that of a *paintbrush* with its two opposite possibilities: depth psychology may either brush society over with its own theoretical colouring, or with masterly brushstrokes re-present society in the form of a truly artistic image. Such an *image* is then neither a photographic copy of society (sociologizing the personal), nor a fantasmic creation unrelated to what it re-presents (psychologizing the social).

In developing this middle position, Samuels draws on diverse sources, from political philosophy and economics, to mythology and spirituality. This diversity of material creates a polymorphous complexity (if not perplexity) which may scandalize the scholarly reader who expects conventionally ordered presentations. However, this paper, like most of Samuels' recent writings, is bubbling with creativity in a way which may intoxicate some readers or perplex others. This is a solo quest where Samuels does not rely on other similar investigations from the literature on this topic and it is, therefore, easy to criticize him for not placing his own contribution in the context of the classic studies in this field within the wide spectrum of depth psychology.

Free Associations (1993) Volume 3, Part 4 (No. 28): 612–16

At this stage, it may be useful to place the paper in the context both of Samuels' own development as an author and the development of analytical psychology today. After providing a systematizing approach to his own field of Jungian analysis with his books *Jung and the Post-Jungians* (1985), *A Critical Dictionary of Jungian Analysis* (with Shorter and Plaut, 1986), and his edited collections *The Father: Contemporary Jungian Perspectives* (1985) and *Psychopathology: Contemporary Jungian Perspectives* (1989), Samuels allowed himself to venture into more innovative themes with *The Plural Psyche* (1989). The present paper (which is part of his new book) pushes his original thinking further into new spheres – those associated with the political dimension. Some of the themes here are continuations of old motifs of his, such as his exaltation of fragmentation and plurality, and his scepticism about the idea of normative development. The political dimension has a broader significance within the field of contemporary Jungian analysis. Following Jung's own ambivalent stance towards the political realm, Jungian analysts seem recently to have begun moving away from their notable passivity and have joined their other analyst colleagues in exploring the political implications of their theory and practice. Samuels has been one of the protagonists of this movement, and this paper represents one of the finest examples of what a Jungian approach can contribute to this exploration.

My own dilemma in responding to this paper lies in the fact that, overall, I find myself in agreement with most of Samuels' ideas. My disagreements lie mainly with the manner in which he puts them across, which I do not find sufficiently systematic and mindful of the methodological implications of his assertions. For example, his thinking challenges the linear and causal-reductive epistemology and favours a more circular and what might be called systemic epistemology. Yet, his identification of the characteristics of his preferred approach is insufficient and his consideration of their theoretical and practical implications non-existent.

Another central argument of his concerns the status of *image*. Towards the end of his paper he refers to the 'the world of imagery' as a 'shared imaginal world that transcends the boundary of private and public'. This appears to be a crucial point of the paper. It is here that he attempts to offer an explanation of the connecting tissue between the two realms. Yet he does not develop this further but, instead, refers the reader to a chapter in his previous book, *The Plural Psyche*. I can understand if the reader would feel cheated here.

In addition to these untidy aspects of the paper, there are a couple of other points which require closer attention. In attacking the normative ideology of developmental psychology and what Samuels calls the 'object relations consensus', he seems also to reject the idea of development altogether. In reacting against the political implications of the ideology of maturity, he seems to throw out the baby with the bathwater. The problem of development is not an easy one because, although I share his concern over the limitations of the normative approaches, one cannot deny the fact that there *is* development in the sense of maturity. For example, there is a definite physiological maturity in a child which is expressed, *inter alia*, in terms of increased co-ordination and integration of functions. In other words, it is sensible to talk about development and maturity in a certain context, and it is dangerous and misleading to do so in another context. Samuels does not make this distinction; neither does he examine the principle behind accommodating such paradoxes. He could have done so had he developed, for example, the principles of systemic epistemology with its essentially paradoxical methodology. Paradox is the only means of addressing simultaneously two different levels of discourse which appear not to be compatible. For example, this occurs when one wishes to give a complete response to a person whose verbal expression is different from its implied or non-verbal meaning. Viewing development paradoxically, one appreciates that not only does the past influence the present, but also that the present influences the past. In order to accept this, one has to move away from a reified notion of development and indeed appreciate it as an *image* and not as a set of historical events. In other words, our image of the past is certainly coloured by our present state.

Closer awareness of the self-reflexive paradoxes involved in this paper would have helped Samuels also to observe his own attempt at resacralization in writing this very article. His own treatment of politics betrays a search for absolute truth, and this search is in itself a form of resacralization. If he accuses the developmental theorists of being gripped by the numinosity of the image of mother and infant, his own approach is dominated by the numinosity of the Trickster. Resacralizing the Trickster is not very different from resacralizing any other image. By applying Samuels' analysis of what happens to resacralizing attempts, we understand that a split occurs which divides the acceptable from the non-acceptable, the positive from the negative. In this sense the paper, by exalting the Trickster, errs on the side of chaos rather than order. This could account for the paper's richness of creativity whereby the ideas introduced are not sufficiently developed.

Another image that comes to mind is that of the prostitute. In Greek-Cypriot folklore the word 'politician' is also used to refer to a prostitute. The connection between the two is that both politicians and prostitutes deal with matters of 'polis', the city, the public domain; both are there to serve and please the citizens all the time. This, of course, implies a *de facto* exclusion of any absolute truth and any resacralization. Thus, the political level of discourse, according to this image, is a purely pragmatic one without any evaluation. It lacks the mobility of the Machiavellian Prince and it includes the Trickster idea but without its numinous qualities.

The personal and political realms are indeed connected by images. This implies a primacy of the realm of images which in a sense precedes both the individual and political structures. In turn, such a primacy of the imaginary implies a particular type of definition of the unconscious, according to which the unconscious is structured by images. Such a definition would bring Jung and Lacan closer together, and in opposition to Freud. There is no emphasis on the Freudian unconscious as being structured, as it is with both the Jungian and Lacanian. Moreover, this idea of images creates a new way of appreciating the collective unconscious as a storehouse of what could be termed *collective structures of meaning*, which is what the images are about. This also may solve the problem of dichotomy between nature and environment at the level of culture. Collective structures of meaning are both 'nature' and 'environment', in so far as they are both 'within' and 'without' the individual. As images, collective structures of meaning have both an independent existence of their own (e.g., in mythology, folklore, etc.) as well as in individuals (as sources of personal meaning).

Finally, returning to the image of the paintbrush, depth psychology may thus relate to culture much like the Heraclitean Delphic oracle which neither 'indicates clearly nor conceals but gives a sign' (Fragment 93).

REFERENCES

Heraclitus (1987) T.M. Robinson, ed. *Fragments*. Toronto: University of Toronto Press.

Samuels, A. (1985) *Jung and the Post-Jungians*. London and Boston, MA: Routledge & Kegan Paul.

—— (ed.) (1985) *The Father: Contemporary Jungian Perspectives*. London: Free Association Books.

—— (ed.) (1989) *Psychopathology: Contemporary Jungian Perspectives*. London: Karnac Books.

—— (1989) *The Plural Psyche: Personality, Morality and the Father*. London and New York: Routledge.

Samuels, A., Shorter, B. and Plaut, A. (1986) *A Critical Dictionary of Jungian Analysis*. London and New York: Routledge & Kegan Paul.

Address for correspondence: 20 Woodriffe Road, London E11 1AH, UK

Reply

Andrew Samuels

K arl Figlio writes in his response that he 'can see what [I] am getting at' and I think the constructive and profound tone of his response shows that this is indeed the case. His call for 'research techniques, literature, training and monitoring' to be introduced into the field of political and cultural analysis is bold and timely, and I agree with it.

Figlio has highlighted the importance, to my way of thinking about culture and politics, of building upon a clinical model without converting cultural and social problematics into either patient or baby. What is central is the adoption of an analytical attitude, but in an as-if format. Clinical method may then turn out to be of more use to cultural and political analysis of a depth-psychological kind than schemas of personality development, models of the structure of the unconscious, or metapsychology. Moreover, this could help to end the isolation of the clinical project of depth psychology from the political world. Figlio and I seem to share the same dream: a politicization of the clinical; clinic as bridge between the personal and the political, not, as so often protrayed, clinic as obstacle to the interplay of personal and political.

What I want to do is to sketch out the reasons why it is clinical theorizing about the countertransference that should engage our interest. I am not forgetting the transference. But if the political/ cultural analyst – or indeed the citizen – is regarded too readily as having a transference to the culture, then, without in any way demeaning the role of the patient in analysis, that citizen or political analyst takes up the role of patient. Given the ubiquity of object relations theory, that role as patient swiftly collapses into the role of being a baby. By proposing that it is the countertransference that carries the burden of political and cultural analysis, I put the citizen in the analyst's chair, with all the maddening mixture of power and powerlessness that that implies. I want us to add the idea that the citizen has the role of the analyst with his or her countertransference to the more obvious notion that the citizen has a transference to political culture.

As we know, the experience of countertransference can be a humbling one. By locating the political referents of the as-if clinical process within the as-if analyst and not within the as-if patient, I intend to problematize the analyst. Hopefully, this will help to reduce the possibility of an arrogant, from-on-high, experience-distant pathologizing of the political – which has marred many previous attempts to link depth psychology and politics.

For the very idea of a countertransference on the part of the political/cultural analyst brings with it the penumbra or residue of neuroticism in the analyst – his or her unresolved neurotic conflicts in relation to politics and culture. Whenever there is an experience of countertransference, there is an uncertainty about whose 'stuff' it is – the analyst's (the citizen's), the patient's (the political problem's), or a mixture of the two.

The goal is to work out a way of translating a subjective response to a cultural or political event into something of use in pragmatic politics. We have to do this in full recognition of the fact that subjectivity is itself partly the result of the political, that subjectivity has arisen and is constructed in part out of the political. In many disciplines, the search for this kind of translation is on; feminism led the way here. For example, the historian Ludmilla Jordanova wrote: 'Historians have little occasion to allow their subjective selves to take part in their work, yet to do so would open vast new territories' (1985, p. 121).

One way of summing up the ideas that are exercising Figlio and me is to take a sentence from a clinical text, such as the following, and rewrite it in a politicized vein: 'It is essential to find some way to put forward for analytic investigation that which is occurring in the analyst as a purely subjective and private experience' (Bollas, 1987, p. 205). This then becomes: 'It is essential to put forward for political investigation that which is occurring in the citizen as a purely subjective and private experience.' If we rewrite like that, then we are some way towards having a methodology that helps us to confront those political events that Figlio is quite right to say are also cultural symbols. (See Samuels, 1992, for a fuller account of countertransference and politics.)

I will conclude my reply to Figlio's response by picking up on a few minor points of disagreement. I think I am aware that splitting is a process and its elements are not concrete or tangible things. That is precisely why I argued for a thorough re-evaluation of the tricksterish phenomenology of splitting. With regard to the dream, I didn't mean to foreclose on other interpretations but to add in a more 'political' one, so that the patient's unconsciously-taken-up political commitments would be made clearer. The images of ether and rhizome were introduced partly to point up the fact that concepts such as projection are themselves images, or riddled with images, and therefore should not be regarded as inherently more sensible, grounded, technical, practical, analytical etc. I can see that providing any image that purports to illuminate processes of unconscious communication was offering a hostage up to fortune! Finally, I am very much aware of the utility and benevolence of judiciously deployed reductionism. This was the conclusion of a chapter on the development of personality in *The Plural Psyche* (Samuels, 1989, pp. 15–47).

I turn now to Sonu Shamdasani's response. I have to say, at the outset, that he and I are both victims of the inevitable long production schedule of a learned journal. Many of my ideas have gone on developing and a friendly debate between him and me has already played a part in that process. I will work through his comments in the order in which he makes them.

I am glad for his support in my critique of object relations as a (potentially hegemonistic) source of an analysis of politics and culture. But I cannot agree that I am replacing 'baby' by 'myth'. In ordinary analytical discourse, one does not deploy 'the baby' in the way I am deploying myth (and legend and Renaissance political theory) in my text. However, to use Figlio's phrase, I can see what he is getting at and I agree that there is a risk of using myth reductively. Incidentally, I am not sure that the provenance of myths interferes with their potential to stimulate imaginative, and ultimately effective engagement with socio-political problematics. Cultural relativism is important but we should not let it become a god. The Trickster theme, leading, as it can, to a discussion of the whole question of factoring the subjective into political discourse, does not, at least in my view, contribute to the political marginalization of women simply because the Trickster cycle arose in a patriarchal culture.

I can readily understand Shamdasani's objections to the passages on 'resacralization', and here I must say that I am not sure he does see what I am getting at. It could be that the problem is connected with the differences between depth psychology and philosophy. Although I am generally in favour of the hybridization of disciplines, there have to be some differences. A depth psychologist has as a credo that he or she is 'in' that which is being analysed, whether patient, political problematic or art work. While some philosophers might pay lip-service to the difficulty of maintaining the observer/observed boundary, often this is not reflected in their texts. So, for Shamdasani, the idea that analysts might somehow be linked up with fundamentalist religion is just too much to stomach. It was hard for me at first, I must confess. But if one's goal, resulting no doubt from identifying oneself as a depth psychologist, is to track and speak up about such connections, no matter how painful, then there is little alternative but to leave such shocking linkages out in the open.

But there are less charged linkages and connections that I am making in this piece. The worldwide importance of questions concerning market economics, including the current claim, emanating from the United States, that such economics constitute the final form of human economic organization, can hardly be denied. It is surely the advantage of a depth-psychological approach that similarities can be denoted when only differences seemed obvious.

In spite of these rebuttals, I think Shamdasani would agree with me that we need more in any analysis of economics from a depth-psychological angle than the simplicities that reduce all of political economy to 'greed', 'envy' and so forth. Economic organization isn't 'primitive' in the sense that some describe the processes of a baby (or a psychotic) as primitive!

Shamdasani has much of interest to say about the concept of the political development of the person.[1] As he knows, my views have changed somewhat from the time I wrote my paper. The idea of political development is intended to be employed as non-normatively and non-judgementally as possible, though it would be as well for me to admit openly that my own political beliefs and values will enter the picture and help to bring a kind of hierarchy into play. This is absolutely unavoidable but I do not believe that having beliefs and values of my own makes me less neutral or different from theorists in the fields of moral, spiritual, religious and personality development who undoubtedly have moral, spiritual, religious, and psychological positions of their own to defend and privilege. Anyway, as Habermas pointed out, theory is different from ideology and knowledge is different from mystification.

My interest is *not* in what might be called 'political maturity'. No such universal exists. My interest is in how people got to where they are politically and, above all, how they themselves think, feel, explain and communicate about how they got to where they are politically; a subjective narrative of political development. Moreover, they may turn out not to be where they thought they were politically, or to have got to where they are by a route that they did not know about. When a patient in analysis, or a comrade in a political struggle, describes his or her political experiences, in the sense of formative or crucial political experiences, we listen with a mix of literal and metaphorical/hermeneutic understandings. Sometimes, the most productive path to follow would be to accept fully the person's account of their political history; at other times, what the person has to say may be understood as image, symbol and metaphor; at other times, as defensive and/or distorted; sometimes, it will be a mélange of these ways of understanding;

sometimes, a competition between them in the mind of the interlocutor.

As Shandasani knows, the idea of development does not have to be used as if it were an exclusively linear, personalistic, causal-deterministic idea, characterized by regularity and predictability. Development is a creative fantasy – and, by fantasy, I do not mean anything pathological or lacking connection to reality. Political development is also a fantasy that enables us to look at an aspect of the person, an area of the psyche, and a dimension of the culture that have been relatively neglected.

Phases of development do not just fade away. Each so-called phase remains active in the psyche in competitive relation to phases which, to the observer, seem to be successive. Therefore, to the concepts of the political development of the person and the political history of the person, I should like to add the concept of 'the political here-and-now of the person'. To give a very simple example: one can ask of a Hampstead liberal how he or she thinks and feels he or she became a Hampstead liberal. (Maybe they'll dispute that label.) We do not have to accept fully what we are told, though that must always remain an option, but are free to dialogue with the narrative (the myth?) we are being given. Maybe the person has no idea how they became a Hampstead liberal, how they got to the place in which they now are, politically speaking. This not knowing can be explored, if the person is willing to do it. As I say, I cannot deny that I have views about Hampstead liberals but that shouldn't stop me trying to facilitate the answering, however partial, of these and other, related, questions.

Recently, I have begun to conduct experiential workshops on the theme of the political development of the person; the first was at the 'Psychoanalysis and the Public Sphere' conference in 1991. These produce fascinating psychological and political material and have aided me in refining my ideas. For example, I feel more confident about the function of primal scene imagery as expressive of what I have referred to above as the political here-and-now of the person. In addition, perplexing questions of 'political style' and the possibility of a person being comfortable with more than one political style have been raised and explored. I will publish an account of these workshops in due course (Samuels, 1993).

I was pleased to have elicited David Mayers' response because it shows so clearly why my paper had to be written.

Mayers organizes things so that he can write from within the safety of two protected redoubts: socialism and Kleinian psychoanalysis. To make his system of fortifications work, and to justify it, he has conjured up the Jungian tribal enemy. I suspect there will be many who will find his particular claims to the ideological possession of socialism and psychoanalysis to be problematic.

Mayers attacks my piece for being naïve, reactionary, perverse, petit-bourgeois and post-modern. He feels that I am out of touch and out of sympathy with the kind of psychoanalytic viewpoint expressed by Money-Kyrle in 'The aim of psycho-analysis' (1971). I thought it would be interesting to work through Money-Kyrle's list to see what light it sheds on the debate between Mayers and me.

When I think of the breast as a supremely beautiful and, to use Money-Kyrle's word, 'good' object, I think about what makes a vision of such beauty possible. Isn't this, in part, the recognition of the breast as having its own life, originating its own beauty, free of controlling (defining) impulses on the part of the baby based on 'social cues, formal qualities and intellectual criteria' (Meltzer, 1988, p. 2)? Do Mayers' tight definitions of socialism and psychoanalysis recognize the capacity of these disciplines to develop, to move on, to inspire new thoughts and actions? Does he see the beauty that stems from their open-mindedness, open-endedness, and their enigmatic resistance to proprietorship?

When I think of the parents in creative intercourse, I think of the human capacity to sustain constructive and creative conflict, whether this is intrapsychic conflict or socio-political conflict (see Samuels, 1989, pp. 123–42). A fertile primal scene requires space for differentiation, dialogue and rebellion. But there is also what I have called a 'stuck' primal scene in which such intercourse, understood on every level, cannot take place. You cannot simply shove your parents together in a forced union, a Mayersian shotgun marriage of socialism and psychoanalysis sanctioned by a suspect logic. In this logic, because psychoanalysis and socialism both work off a substructure/superstructure hypothesis, their desired goals must be the same. Hence, socialism and depressive position are one. This parthenogenetic move of Mayers' is, to use Money-Kyrle's words, 'a megalomanic delusion' (1971, p. 442). The tangible outcome of creative parental union is a baby and this makes me think of the need to respect and protect new life and new things in general.

When I think about accepting the inevitability of death, I think of the corollary need to celebrate life when one has it. This means a passionate yet socially responsible engagement with the erotic and sensual dimensions of life, art, religion, tradition, the life of the intellect, and play. Grey is not the only colour.

Worked through like this, I contend that my paper is closer to the ideals expressed in 'The aim of psycho-analysis' than this response.

Mayers' conception of socialism displays the same rigidity as his conception of psychoanalysis. I am not one of those who think that socialism is dead but, in company with many others, I recognize that we have to try to think in terms of there being a plurality of socialisms, each resisting the hegemonistic impulses of the other brands, but all somehow linked. As Karl Kautsky put it in 1918, 'Socialism as such is not our goal, which is rather the abolition of every kind of exploitation or oppression, be it directed against a class, a party, a sex, or a race' (quoted in Blackburn, 1991, p. 7). To achieve these ends, I agree with those who argue that socialist thought has to engage with what is implied by the market. It seems to me that socialism is already moving on to do just that. Hence, what is needed (if anything at all is needed) from psychoanalysis is a contribution concerning the depth psychology of the market. Psychoanalytic critiques of the market should expose what R.W. Johnson called the 'warmed-over wishfulness of so many on the left' (1992).

In my paper I did not say that we 'chose' capitalism but that people are invested in certain ways in maintaining economic inequality. Nor did I assume that, in a bargaining or negotiating situation, everyone starts from the same place. The psychosocial consequences of the destruction of free collective bargaining in Britain have been immense. But it is amazing how often current left-wing texts, for instance in *New Left Review*, return to the question of the 'socialized market', meaning some way of factoring compassion, social justice and alterity into market economics.

Mayers writes as if a body of texts exists to give a satisfactory and satisfying account of the relations between a class-based analysis of social and economic conditions, and an unconscious phantasy-based analysis of the internal world. It is this assumption that seems to justify his accusation that I am somehow ignoring the economic facts of life. But my text displays what will be, for some readers, an almost relentless concentration on economics, if not in the language that Mayers says I should have used. My paper constitutes a Hermetic attempt to recover the idea of the market from capitalism and make a contribution to notions of a socialized market.

Perhaps the Left will have to be content with a more modest role. As Habermas put it, socialism will become 'the radically reformist self-criticism of a capitalist society which, in the form of constitutional democracy with universal suffrage and a welfare state, has developed not only weaknesses but also strengths' (quoted in Lukes, 1992).

Here is the basis for a freely-entered-into marriage between psychoanalysis and socialism, for such modest but important goals could be shared by both partners. The sketchy beginning of an expanded version of 'the political' that I was attempting in my piece could constitute a sort of marriage bed for this project.

I do not have the space to do more than demur at Mayers' version of true psychoanalysis. For example, Mayers' remarks about the baby–breast relationship show up the kind of numinous, fascinated involvement I was writing about. It is unclear how he expects us to read him: literally, metaphorically, both, neither? (See Samuels, 1989, pp. 15–47 for a fuller discussion of this topic.)

I conclude like this: in his pseudo-authoritative privileging of the internal world, his reductive deployment of the idea of innate, unconscious phantasy, his rejection of the role of social and cultural factors in the construction of the unconscious, I have to inform David Mayers that he resembles nothing so much as a Classical Jungian analyst, of the kind I have spent much of my working life arguing against! A politics based on these features must lead to what Bob Young has called 'a political culture that is so conscience-driven and unrewarding that people will burn out in it' (1991, p. 513).[2]

What Renos Papadopoulos has to say about 'collective structures of meaning' and the 'primacy of the imaginary' indicates that analytical psychology is not the fossil portrayed by David Mayers. However, Papadopoulos' statement that 'the unconscious is structured by images' will no doubt bring the weight of intellectual orthodoxy crashing down on his head. Nevertheless, in spite of the problems with such a statement, Papadopoulos shows us that images have a cutting edge and a capacity to debate and dialogue with each other that is every bit as fine as the more usually valued debate and dialogue of ideas. He pits his Prostitute against my Trickster and, if we allow the intercourse of those two, novel understandings about the destiny of 'the Politician' may emerge.

Papadopoulos' own challenge to the mores of the academy should, viewed logically, have led him to something other than the antithesis between scholarly and imaginative writing which he presents as a problem with my piece. I find myself wondering why this opposition continues to exist in the way that it does. I cannot persuade myself that my piece is closer to a poem than to a theoretical text. Therefore, I suggest that what is needed is a more generous conception of what is scholarly in writing. This would not by itself protect me from the valid criticism that I should have placed my text in a more fleshed-out context and I certainly plan to remedy that omission. But I do not want to lose sight of the possibility that we are on the verge of a revolution in our understanding of what constitutes scholarly, academic and intellectual writing. We already know that many, apparently discursive, texts in the human sciences are full of rhetoric. I do not see why Papadopoulos (and others) cannot extend the warmth of his systemic epistemology to embrace the paradox that scholarship may be carried by other than scholarly writings, and that imaginative productivity may constitute a means of expression for the intellect.

En passant, I want to say that this question of scholarly versus imaginative writing is something that *Free Associations* itself might wish to dwell upon. It is, at one and the same time, a question of style and something more.

It is undeniably the case that, at times, I slip into the sorts of habits that, officially, I am arguing against. I think that it is more or less inevitable that I should have become fascinated by Trickster. But even from within this merged state I can protest at the easy equation made by Papadopoulos of Trickster and chaos. If that equation holds, then, obviously, anything non-Trickster is bound to be orderly. But what Papadopoulos has overlooked is that there are subdivisions to be made within the categories of 'chaos' and 'order'. We have to learn to speak in terms of tricksterish chaos – different from other forms of chaos, for instance the chaos caused by command economies. Then there would be tricksterish order – different from other forms of order, for instance the psychological order caused by an overclear application of stereotyped ideas about gender. To put it conversationally, some chaos is good and some order is bad, and sometimes good chaos will become bad chaos and good order will become bad order.

I will conclude with an appreciation of what Papadopoulous writes about development because, in spite of what he writes about my having rejected the concept, I think we are in overall agreement. The discipline of depth psychology needs urgently to get to grips with the multi-faceted nature of its core idea of development. This would include an apperception of the historical-causal, metaphorical, and teleological aspects of development. Moreover, it won't be enough to *list* the diverse facets of developmental theory.

These theories really want to argue with each other and depth psychologists should carefully tend the plant of debate, dialogue and argument. That is why the emergence of consensus is not at all the sensible and progressive step that it seems to be; far from it. Stilling the debates about development by proclaiming the coming into being of a consensus injures the psyche and, hence, injures humanity. Thus the argumentative politics of our profession merge with the argumentative politics of our world.

NOTES

1 I am aware that there are problems with my (or anyone's) use of the term 'person'. I think that the need to retain the idea of the person is pressing when we consider the political dimensions of life. To continue to refer to the person is not as naïve as it seems. It does not bring with it a belief in an innate, single viewpoint, arising from a heart or core or centre, as if independent of social institutions, social relations and language. In fact, my usage of the idea of the person involves precisely the recognition that the person is indeed constructed, polyvalent and heterogeneous. Else why bring the person into politics at all? The deconstruction of the person is not the same as the deconstruction of the political – and the political constellates the person living in the polis.

Paradoxically, this speculation of mine about the political development of the person is part of, not in opposition to, attempts to 'decentre the habitual focus of psychoanalysis on an individual [by] evoking the place of the between, thus dissolving the logic of inner and outer' (Oakley, 1989, pp. 3–5).

I am not forgetting the wounded and grieving nature of the late modern or post-modern person. Today, there is scarcely the possibility of a person divorced from a sense of woundedness and an accompanying grief. That is why these are matter for healers.

2 Young's alternative – 'radical wine-tasting parties' (1991, p. 513) – presents us with a false set of alternatives!

REFERENCES

Blackburn, R (1991) 'Socialism after the Crash', New Left Review, 185: 5–68.

Bollas, C. (1987) The Shadow of the Object: Psychoanalysis and the Unthought Known. London: Free Association Books.

Johnson, R.W. (1992) Review of C. Lemke and G. Marks, eds The Crisis of Socialism in Europe. Duke University Press. In London Review of Books, 12 March 1992.

Jordanova, L. (1985) 'Fantasy and history in the study of childhood', Free Associations 2: 110–22.

Lukes, S. (1992) Review of Robin Blackburn, ed. After the Fall: The Failure of Communism and the Future of Socialism. London: Verso. In New Statesman and Society, 6 March 1992.

Meltzer, D. (1988) *The Apprehension of Beauty*. Strath Tay: Clunie Press.

Money-Kyrle, R. (1971) 'The aim of psycho-analysis', in D. Meltzer, ed. *Collected Papers of Roger Money-Kyrle*. Strath Tay: Clunie Press, 1978.

Oakley, C. (1989) 'Introducing an incomplete project', in Robin Cooper and others, *Thresholds between Philosophy and Psychoanalysis: Papers from the Philadelphia Association*. London: Free Association Books, pp. 1–14.

Samuels, A. (1989) *The Plural Psyche: Personality, Morality and the Father*. London and New York: Routledge.

—— (1992) 'Countertransference and politics', *British Journal of Psychotherapy* 9: 40–63.

—— (1993) *The Political Psyche*. London and New York: Routledge, forthcoming.

Young, R. (1991) 'Psychoanalytic critique of productivism', *Free Associations* 2: 507–14.

Address for correspondence: 17 Archibald Road, London N7 0AN, UK

FORTHCOMING FROM FREE ASSOCIATION BOOKS

WHY MEN HATE WOMEN

by Adam Jukes

Adam Jukes works with men who are abusive and violent to women. In the last five years he has been involved in the London Men's Centre, which offers dedicated programmes to men who are violent. He began working with abusive men as a psychodynamic psychotherapist, but as his work continued he found that the work of feminists in the refuge movement and in the 'speaking bitterness' literature could not be ignored. He has attempted to integrate these two perspectives in his work.

He believes that violence is simply the most visible of a continuum of methods of abuse which men inflict on women, which is designed to establish and maintain control of them in both institutions and personal relationships. He knows that the way in which he presents men in this book will generate distress for those men who experience their masculinity as a burden. He argues that misogyny, the hatred of women, is an inescapable element in the development of masculinity. He explores feminist constructions of male violence and dominance, and psychoanalytic accounts of the development of male gender identity.

This is a shocking book. Drawing widely on recent writings from the men's and women's movements, and from the psychoanalytic literature, Adam Jukes offers a disturbing, thought-provoking view of the issues which will be of interest to mental health professionals and all concerned readers.

c.256 pages pb 1 85343 195 8 £15.95

THE UNDISCOVER'D COUNTRY

New Essays on Psychoanalysis and Shakespeare
Edited by B.J.Sokol

This collection of essays, drawing together new material from four countries, challenges many of the current trends in Shakespeare studies.

The discussions of Shakespeare's plays and poems in this collection, by a range of academics, practsing psychotherapists and the theatre director Jonathan Miller, discover many kinds of reference beyond the text: intuitable meanings, symbolisms inspired by the dark - undiscover'd - side of human relations, and characterizations of individual and group identities. The authors - Philip K. Bock, M.D. Faber, Jonathan Miller, Ruth Nevo, Angela Sheppard, B.J. Sokol and Lyn Stephens - are especially interested in the dynamics of emotional life. They variously bring to bear on Shakespeare's texts knowledge of theatrical practice, social history, anthropology, theology, political history, art history and other disciplines.

The editor contributes an introduction which claims the importance of psychological and psychodynamic understanding for the progress of literary studies. The volume also contains a bibliography of psychoanalytic and psychological Shakespeare studies in English from 1979-1989, which will prove invaluable to those already familiar with the two previous ten-year bibliographies in the field.

B.J. Sokol lectures in English at Goldsmiths' College, University of London. He has published recently on Sir Philip Sidney, Shakespeare, Jonson, Milton and Marvell.

272 pages pb 1 85343 197 4 £14.95

FURTHER REFLECTIONS ON JUNG

The Jung–Klein hybrid

Michael Fordham

The title of this paper is derived from a formula, invented by A.B. Plaut when he was in the United States, to explain to Jungians in California something of what was taking place in London, i.e. that we were being strongly influenced by Klein's discoveries. The phrase has been used mostly in an unfavourable sense, but Plaut was a rose-grower and he would know that hybrid tea roses were among the most beautiful in existence.

I myself had been influential in interesting Jungians in Klein for the following reasons. In the thirties I was attempting to treat children at the London Child Guidance Clinic; there I was confronted with the fact that Jungians were not only indifferent to problems of childhood but also positively antagonistic to the analysis of children. Jung did leave us a sketchy theory of development, but there was no technique for the analysis of children: he thought that a child's deviation from the normal was mostly to be laid at the door of his parents whose unconscious conflicts influenced him unfavourably. He did, however, treat some latency and pre-adolescent children using a method reminiscent of Alfred Adler: he emphasized the ego and the child's tasks in life, thus avoiding analysis of unconscious processes. Apart from these few cases, he recorded observations on a small girl, Ann by name

Free Associations (1993) Volume 3, Part 4 (No. 28): 631–41

(Jung, 1909). It was a companion piece to Freud's Little Hans (Freud, 1909) but Jung laid far more emphasis than Freud on cognitive development and the use of symbols as a stimulus to thought about sexuality. He was already laying emphasis on the symbol as lying at the root of ongoing processes.

His theory of archetypes and of the collective unconscious, which came later, and his idea of the ego as the centre of consciousness all seemed to be ideas which might be used to facilitate the study of childhood. That I proceeded to do even though Jung's primary interest lay in the so-called second half of life: he emphasized archetypal manifestations and the inner world of imagination leading to individuation in that period. In so doing he left a large gap, since he did not apply his theory to childhood. That, I thought, was a space which I could attempt to fill in.

Other than observation, however, there were inadequate techniques to employ. So at first I simply encouraged the children under my care at the clinic to draw, paint and tell me their dreams. In that material I found quite frequent archetypal fantasies, i.e., dreams and pictures depicting witches, giants, fairy tale and other mythological figures. There was nothing surprising in that, but paying attention to them did not have the deleterious effect which Jung, his follower Frances Wickes (1927) and most Jungian analysts supposed would result. Further than this, children showing pathological features benefited without parents investigating their unconscious processes, which Jungian theory required.

So I began to think that the child psyche was far more structured than I had assumed and that the archetypes were acting in childhood very much as they did in more mature people. These conclusions made analysis in childhood a serious possibility.

It was then that I discovered Melanie Klein, and was surprised at the findings she presented in *The Psycho-Analysis of Children* (1932). I reflected that the infant's relation to his mother's body and her insides was comparable to the hero's journey into the underworld or being swallowed by a monster – compare Jonah and the whale, which Jung had analysed in relation to the drive to enter into the mother for rebirth. Yet it was clear that small children did not talk the language of mythology; they expressed themselves basically in terms of bodies or parts of them. I tried using these terms and found that my relation to small children improved, especially severely disturbed ones whom we now call autistic or psychotic – I felt on the right track.

Julia, two-and-a-half years old, showed me more. She was referred to me because of fits in which she became unconscious, and she showed other symptoms of regression such as clinging to her mother and being quite incapable of relating to other people including her sister. Since she was unable to separate much from her mother, I sat the mother outside the playroom; leaving the door open I induced the child to come into it. Together we made plasticine models of a mother which she smashed to pieces; then she ran out of the room to her real mother. Having made contact with her she returned to the playroom. I had told her that mother was broken and inferred that she ran outside to ascertain whether that was true or not. After a time the play changed and she broke up babies. At this time her mother told me that she had become fascinated with babies and if she saw a perambulator, when shopping with her mother, was not to be satisfied until she had looked into it and saw what was inside it. I will not go further into the details of the girl's play except to say that she eventually broke up the mother and baby and then repaired the couple and that she changed out of all recognition: her fits stopped, she became a lively independent child who could enjoy life. I heard five years later that her development had been most satisfactory, and among other indications of progress was the fact that she had gone to school and enjoyed it.

Then there was the question of transference. Julia evidently felt safe enough to express her feelings and impulses in no uncertain terms. If that were a transference it would be of a very primitive kind, a feeling of being held and secure with verbal acknowledgement of what she had done. That made it possible for her to distinguish her fantasy from reality and eventually discover that she could recreate the destroyed mother and baby of her inner world through symbolic play – all good Jungian stuff, illustrating the very early activity of archetypes, the formation of symbols, the inner world and a growing capacity to distinguish her actions in the playroom from reality.

I did not make any transference interpretations which might have run 'Doctor-mummy safe to break up, real mummy in danger', but I did so with other, older children who could talk: it helped the treatment forward. All that was in line with Kleinian experience, so the ground was set for cross-fertilization. It was, however, a case of my being fertilized by Klein and not much the other way round. Yet Kleinians did listen and one expressed warm appreciation of my exposition after a symposium on countertransference.

In the meantime I had got the idea that Jung's formulations about the self might be useful. This idea derived from the observations I have been describing, which showed that children were in important respects separate beings with an inner world of their own which they built up. Then I came across what Jung called mandala figures (circular images with variable content), and especially a series of them which Frieda Fordham showed me: they had been painted by a small girl who had been evacuated during the war and was caught in sex play; she was promptly returned home as a public danger – she became confused and disoriented but, while painting these pictures, recovered.

My interest was greatly stimulated because Jung had understood this type of symbol as representing the self, so I studied how often mandala symbols occurred in infancy and small children: they were common and often seemed to be a basis for the construction of a body image. Circular scribbles were also a prominent feature; they appeared to exercise control over bad objects, and were used to protect good ones or were related to self-assertive actions. One infant particularly fascinated me: he was a one-year-old who became absorbed in making them on a wall. When he discovered the word 'I', he stopped drawing those forms.

Now Jung's formulation conceived the self differently from current notions. It was not a part of the ego and was larger than the ego and archetypes put together; it transcended opposites, for example, good and bad, or conscious and unconscious, and so was essentially the ultimate organizer of the psyche. Its analogue in Kleinian metapsychology was Bion's '0'. I now made a speculative leap: I postulated that there was an original form of the self which was a psychosomatic entity. It had a firm boundary like the body and organized the elements within. Yet it must act to bring an infant into relation with its mother or parts of her. It must deintegrate as well as integrate. I published that speculation in 1946, but it did not develop for lack of a means for observing babies. Indeed it was not until I studied the mother–infant observations made by students in training in child analysis in 1987 that I found my speculation grew. It could begin to change from an abstract proposition into sequences of states which could be described.

Turning from child therapy to the analysis of adults. In the 1930s training in Jungian methods consisted in the future analyst's own analysis and reading of Jung's own works – especially his seminars. It was thought that our main work applied to borderline cases or ambulant schizophrenics, and persons in the second half of life. Analysis in the psychoanalytic sense might be used, but was only part of the delineation and fostering of the ongoing process of individuation. I myself did not treat schizophrenics or other psychotics, except children. It was this class of patient that most classical Freudians regarded as beyond the reach of psychoanalysis. The Kleinians, however, were evidently encroaching on our field with their emphasis on unconscious fantasy and internal objects. They had a different idiom but there was a rather close analogy. In 1949 that was found to be the case when a symposium was held at the Medical Section of the British Psychological Society on 'Archetypes and internal objects', and the matter was discussed between Jungians and Kleinians.

By then much water had flowed under the bridge: Jungians in London had become much more interested in analytic work, especially in the transference and countertransference, and that brought us even closer to the Kleinians – we could agree with much of what they were saying. Their method, in appearing much more imaginative than classical psychoanalysis, could help us in developing our own techniques which were rudimentary.

Our attention centred on the countertransference. This was not much mentioned in the Jungian literature, although Jung had considered the relation between analyst and patient as interactional: he claimed that the analyst was as much in analysis as the patient – a formulation which was in need of refinement, but expressed an attitude that was to become more important, especially in the more difficult narcissistic and borderline cases. He further understood that a patient could invade and take over the analyst, citing cases in which that had taken place in therapists who came for treatment to him presenting psychotic symptoms; when that state of affairs was identified the therapist could return to normal. So when Klein (1955) described projective identification there was a selectively responsive audience among Jungians, of whom I was one. I incorporated the idea in a paper called 'Technique and countertransference', in which I postulated that projective and introjective identifications went on unconsciously in any analytic process and that these affected the analyst: they formed the basis for thoughts about the patient called interpretations. This notion was like that previously expressed by Paula Heimann when she wrote on countertransference.

In the 1950s I became especially interested in patients who apparently could not use interpretations and who, while attending for treatment regularly, would spend their time making it clear that my efforts to help them were of no use or a waste of time. Sometimes there was a clear theme held with delusional intensity: one woman came because, she claimed, I was in love with her, she did not need analysis, and it was I who kept the interviews going because I could not bear the thought of separation from her. Another one considered that I was afraid of being myself and defended myself by dispensing so-called analysis. It was I who needed treatment for my infantile anxieties and she would continue coming as she thought I was gaining benefit from her presence. I understood these clinical phenomena as due to projection – now I would call it projective identification – but the second of these patients induced complex feelings in me, basically of persecutory depression and helplessness. Both these patients were exceptionally able people, and after their treatment had ended progressed well in their professions. The first case got so far as to acknowledge her love for me; the second one developed into a friend with a rich personal and professional life. I came to understand such cases as exhibiting defences of the self mainly because of the life-and-death quality of their battle, but they also exhibited signs of a delusional transference which could find a resolution by being contained, and eventually interpreted. I thought that it was desirable not to capitulate but to go on sustaining my analytic attitude. Only thus could the destructive attack on my interpretations, and on analysis as a whole, be seen not to have destroyed what I valued. In that way, I thought, I could account for their remarkably regular attendance: they seemed to value my continued existence highly.

Now Jung had said that if a patient has an effect on you, which the second patient had, there must be a hook on which the projection can hang. So what was the hook? I did not think that it was the reproach that interpretations were remote from the patient's feeling which affected me, because I had plenty of that in my first Jungian analysis and had, up to a point, accommodated myself to my analyst's theoretical interest in the material I produced. That was in sharp contrast to my second analyst, who always spoke out of herself and was felt by me to do so. That led on to an interest in the way my interventions were made, rather than in their correctness or otherwise. But I had not integrated these two analyses.

Once again Jung was helpful. He had considerable scepticism about theories: 'Theories are the very devil', he said; and a patient should not be treated according to a preconceived theory. It was necessary to make a new theory for each patient. Also he depreciated an analyst knowing the answer beforehand. He even called that a trick of doctors, referring, I believe rather unfairly, to the doctor's diagnosis, which a psychotherapist should seek to avoid.

All these statements by Jung are exaggerations, but they helped me build up a formula about arriving at an interpretation which was not based on theory but came out of the self. That involves trusting one's unconscious, in which projective and introjective identifications are active. When teaching students I express the attitude required for that to take place as follows. In your seminars you will have accumulated much knowledge about the treatment of patients – all that you must try to lock up in a mental filing cabinet: divesting yourself of all knowledge, memory and desire (cf. also Bion, 1970) you must look and listen to your patient as though you have never seen him before so you will not have any knowledge of him. In that way you will be open to him and be in the best position to experience his state of mind today. As you listen you will begin to experience his mood and then have some thoughts or feelings, etc. about him. It is out of that that an intervention will arise. I recognize that this formulation is almost impossible to achieve but it can be approximated to. Employing it I have worked with a patient who expresses almost total denial that interpretations and indeed analysis as a whole have done him any good; but he has never attacked either of them as being out of touch with him by reason of presuppositions imposed by me.

Such an observation makes one consider whether total denial produced by the patient is not due to errors in technique or failures to understand the patient. It is, indeed, quite possible for an analysis to embark on an understanding which is not the right one, or insufficiently correct, so that the patient feels you are out of touch. I am sure that the patient's sense that the analyst is in touch is central – recognition by the analyst that he is estranged from his patient, or has not addressed the destructive core with which the patient is struggling, can do a lot to restore the relation between the two and the sense of still being partners in a joint endeavour. It dissolved an impasse in a patient who regularly complained that I had not resolved his pain of struggling with his destructive violence; I recognized that what he said was true because we had not yet been able to uncover its nature. Those of you who are familiar with Rosenfeld's study, *Impasse and Interpretation* (1987), will recognize how close I have come to his position: that these patients struggle with a monstrously destructive demon, the death instinct; that the work has to be done in terms of projective identification; and so it is especially important that the analyst pay close attention to his own emotional responses to his patient – working these out through using his capacity for thought. Rosenfeld also gives valuable attention to whether the analyst has truly listened to his patient's communication on any particular occasion. If he has not done so an impasse may arise, perhaps due to the analyst's making plausible interpretations that have too high a theoretical content. The damage may be very difficult to repair unless the fault is recognized.

Rosenfeld emphasizes the importance of envy as evoking the full power of the death instinct and I am impressed by the explanatory power of that combination and the good use to which he puts it, but I now want to turn to other considerations of a Jungian kind. When I first began to take up the conflicts under consideration I did so with a more apparently positive proposition: that the seemingly negative manifestations had a positive meaning. I assumed that the attack on some (sometimes escalating to all) of the analyst's interventions was due to the pressure to succeed previously exerted by parents and their surrogates on the patient. Consequently the patient's success – and it was sometimes considerable – was experienced as not his own achievement but as one induced by them. An indicator of that in one patient was that when praised, he thought that he had played a trick. His headmaster once praised him highly, but my patient asserted that the man was of very poor quality and quite incapable of assessing him correctly. Anything that smelled of external influence had to be devalued: it was the true self that acted, to all appearances destructively, in order to preserve those elements (self-representations) of itself that remained intact. I should underline here that I refer to the self in Jung's sense; which in my conception would deintegrate into equally destructive and creative components analogous to Freud's life and death instincts.

In order to recover or integrate the good, creative, loving parts of the self it follows that a regression may be necessary according to Jung's assertion that regression has a positive aspect and leads to rebirth. If a result is achieved that can take place: the patient's way of life undergoes considerable alteration, and gains in meaning when the previous, unsatisfactory ways of adaptation have been abandoned. The risk that a reconstruction of the personality may take place has, however, to be envisaged and the analyst may then be landed with a permanent patient.

Jung seldom produced detailed case studies but instead wrote in metaphors. Two of these spring to mind. One concerns the characteristic of the alchemical figure Mercurius whom Jung understands as a manifestation of the self:

The elusive, deceptive, ever-changing content that possesses the patient like a demon now flits from patient to doctor and, as a third party in the alliance continues its game, sometimes impish and teasing, sometimes really diabolical. The alchemists aptly presonified it as the wily god of revelation, Hermes or Mercurius; and, though they lament over the way he hoodwinks them, they still give him the highest names, which bring him very near to deity. (Jung, 1946, p. 188)

The second is the account of the treatment of a king who has lost his vigour and has become ill. The Egyptian physicians were called in. Being alchemists they 'tore the king into little pieces, ground them to powder, mixed them in their "moistening" medicines and put the king back into his heated chamber'. The procedure was repeated but ended up with a dead king. After that the Alexandrian physicians were brought in: they proceeded in much the same way but the 'medicines' were different, and the king rose from the dead 'and cried with a loud voice: "Where are my enemies? I shall kill them all if they do not submit to me" ' (Jung, 1955–6, p. 167).

It is common practice among Jungians to use such material in amplification of material brought by patients. That I seldom do. On one occasion, however, to a patient who persistently derided my interventions, substituting literary matter in place of them, I quoted the account of the king and the alchemical physicians. I underlined the transference significance, i.e., that in pounding my ideas to dust he was hoping that I would one day come up with something significant. That made him laugh, and I think he knew that I was being ironically malicious for I had previously been malicious about a common acquaintance and told him so. On that occasion, early on in his analysis, my confession had made him think that I must be all right for him to come to, since I could be so comfortable with my malice!

NOTE

This essay will subsequently be published in *The Jung–Klein Hybrid*, edited by Barry and Karren Proner.

REFERENCES

Bion, W. (1970) *Attention and Interpretation.* London: Tavistock.

Freud, S. (1909) 'Analysis of a phobia in a five-year-old boy', in James Strachey, ed. *The Standard Edition of the Complete Psychological Works of Sigmund Freud*, 24 vols. London: Hogarth, 1953–73, vol. 10, pp. 1–149.

Jung, C.G. (1909) 'Psychic conflicts in a child', rev. version, *Collected Works* 17.

—— (1946) 'Psychology of the transference', *Collected Works* 16.

—— (1954) *The Development of the Personality. Collected Works* 17.

—— (1955–6) *Mysterium Coniunctionis. Collected Works* 14.

—— (1968) *Psychology and Alchemy. Collected Works* 12.

Klein, M. (1932) *The Psycho-Analysis of Children. The Writings of Melanie Klein*, vol. 2. London: Hogarth, 1980.

—— (1955) 'On identification', *Envy and Gratitude. The Writings of Melanie Klein*, vol. 3. London: Hogarth, 1980.

Rosenfeld, H. (1987) *Impasse and Interpretation.* London: Hogarth.

Wickes, F. (1927) *The Inner World of Childhood.* New York: Appleton.

Address for correspondence: Severalls, Wilton Lane, Jordans, Beaconsfield, Bucks HP9 2RE, UK

Freud and Jung

Margaret Arden

This paper has been adapted from a talk given to a small group of psychoanalysts in May 1990 with the aim of stimulating discussion about the relationship between psychoanalytic ideas and the changing intellectual climate in which we live. I have written several papers on the theme of the need to find a new paradigm for psychoanalysis which would release us from the constraints of Freud's 19th-century scientific thinking. I was influenced both by analysts who used ideas from outside psychoanalysis and also by the many holistic theories that have become popular in recent years. The point of a holistic theory is that it combines scientific and non-scientific ideas into a single world view. Science is not devalued, but it is placed in a wider context in which other viewpoints are not criticized for being non-scientific.

My first paper was about Bateson and Matte Blanco; the second was about holistic thinking as exemplified by David Bohm's theory of implicate order (Bohm, 1980); then I wrote a paper on femininity based on Sylvia Payne's 1935 paper (Arden, 1984, 1985, 1987). The idea of feminine thinking as integrative and holistic originated with Marjorie Brierley and has been around in the Independent Group of the British Psycho-Analytical Society ever since. I suggested that Jung's view of femininity in men and women accords much better with cultural and aesthetic experience than

Free Associations (1993) Volume 3, Part 4 (No. 28): 642–54

Freud's. I also suggested that the yin and yang concept of male and female values could be applied to primary and secondary process.

The concepts of primary and secondary process have undergone considerable change since they were first formulated by Freud. The name 'primary process' denotes that this is the kind of thinking we are born with – in which instincts and affects predominate – in contrast to 'secondary-process', rational thinking which has to be learned. Dreams are the royal road to the unconscious because they are conscious manifestations of the primary-process thinking which forms the boundless sea of the unconscious mind. However, Freud's aim of creating a science of the mind led him to overvalue rationality. The changes in thinking that have taken place since Freud have changed the way we see his work. The imaginative and intuitive aspects of his work are now more apparent than formerly, and we have more understanding of how small a part rational thinking plays in the lives of ordinary people.

The unifying theme in all this is the need to describe the change that has taken place in the way we think about the role of primary process. It is now more than thirty years since Charles Rycroft pointed out that psychoanalysis is a semantic theory, not a scientific one (Rycroft, 1956). Many Independent analysts share this view, and yet the muddle of accepting supposedly scientific statements without demur continues. Bateson wrote that rigour and imagination are the two great contraries of mental life which need to be kept in balance (Bateson, 1980). Bateson did not use the distinction between unconscious and conscious, but his way of describing the duality of the mind has considerable potential for linking psychoanalytic thought with other disciplines. In particular, this way of conceptualizing the relationship of primary and secondary process is a development of Freud's original formulations, which makes it easier to speak about the use of imagination in scientific activity.

In addition it echoes Suzanne Langer's concept of discursive and non-discursive symbolism (Langer, 1942). Langer wrote: 'The great contribution of Freud to the philosophy of mind has been the realisation that human behaviour is not only a food-getting strategy, but also a language; that every move is at the same time a gesture, (p. 51). She elaborated a thesis that the various 'impractical', apparently unbiological activities of man, such as religion, magic, art, dreaming and symptom formation, are basic human activities: 'The essential act of thought is symbolisation. We do not surpass animals in our perceptual skills but in our capacity to transfer perception into ideas. It is this capacity which accounts for those human traits which animals lack: ritual, art, laughter, weeping, speech, superstition and scientific genius' (p. 43). What follows can be attributed to the influence of these ideas on successive generations of the Independent Group, several of whom have written about symbolism.

This outlook is one in which scientific enquiry is seen as one aspect of the range of human activities, and cannot be separated from them in a general discussion of mind. I have become increasingly convinced that the so-called scientific attitude in psychoanalysis is a serious limitation. It is a mistake to think that science can explain everything in psychoanalysis, and it is a grave disservice to Freud to think that he was only a scientist. It was inevitable that Freud used the rigour of science as a basis for his theory; psychoanalysis could not have developed in any other way. In the cause of science Freud had to reject those of his followers who were insufficiently disciplined in their thinking. This was a great loss, particularly in the case of Jung. I have called this paper 'Freud and Jung' because I think that we are still suffering from the idea that Freud was right and Jung was wrong. I wouldn't want Jung without Freud, but I think many of his ideas are valuable, and complementary to Freud's.

It is my contention that analysts suffer from a kind of arrested development when they try to remain loyal to Freud's concept of science. In the same way that we can see the value of 19th-century scientific discoveries while knowing that knowledge has progressed since then, it should be possible to have a double vision of Freud's work, holding in mind both its amazing originality and its historical limitations. For example, it does not matter that Breuer and Freud used the reflex arc to demonstrate the mechanism of hysteria (Freud, 1893). We cannot see this as a valid scientific theory, but we can value the metaphorical significance of the attempt and the bold, imaginative leap that Freud made. My concern is that we do not have any conceptual framework for identifying those areas where Freud was actually wrong.

A holistic paradigm would make it unnecessary to label theories right and wrong, and would make it possible to accept and to integrate Jungian concepts instead of repudiating them. I have always felt sympathy for Jung because he stuck to his guns and refused to be intimidated by Freud in spite of the great cost to himself. Jungians have an advantage over Freudians in that their basic theory is a holistic one, embracing myth and religion and cultural values. They can respond freely to the paradigm changes which are happening in the world, since they do not think of themselves as scientists. The other side of the coin is their lack of rigour; they borrow freely from psychoanalysis whenever they need to.

It seems to me that there is a historical irony, as well as a profound paradox, in the idea of psychoanalysis as a science. Freud's discoveries were about the irrational part of human nature which is not amenable to science as usually understood; and furthermore, science does not admit of paradoxes. The idea that psychoanalytic investigation can lead to a scientific theory is fundamentally unscientific. Fortunately this statement is also historically limited by the profound changes that have taken place in science this century. We tend to overlook the fact that Freud's science is completely outdated because the cause-and-effect outlook on life is still prevalent. Newtonian physics still provides satisfactory explanations for most of the phenomena of everyday life.

When particle physicists discovered that there are limits to certainty about the nature of matter they turned to Zen Buddhism and other Eastern philosophies to find ways of describing their findings. The discoveries of relativity and quantum mechanics meant that the Newtonian universe ceased to be a valid metaphor. The holistic world view that preceded the Enlightenment in the West, and the cyclical world views of Eastern philosophy took on a new relevance. These changes also give greater credibility to Jung's views, which were never confined by causality. It is now possible to think of science and religion as alternative metaphors for explaining the universe. George Trevelyan once said that the physicist's bubble chamber is the modern equivalent of the alembic of the alchemists, wherein man sees his own soul. The trouble with the concept of psychoanalysis as science is that it cannot address the primary importance of meaning. Papers written by Independents in recent years are increasingly concerned with this area. I shall discuss this in a general way and then give some examples.

Since I wrote my paper about David Bohm's implicate order his ideas have been taken up more widely in this country and he has become, inevitably, a cult figure in the USA; he was recently elected a Fellow of the Royal Society. The Jungian analyst Louis Zinkin wrote a paper at the same time as mine, in which he demonstrated the harmony and compatibility of Bohm's holistic theory with Jung's psychology (Zinkin, 1984). More recently I have read a book which spells out in detail the connection between implicate order and synchronicity. This book, by the physicist F. David Peat (1988), explores the myth of causality and shows that a great deal of faith is involved in our belief that cause and effect govern our lives. Even if we accept a reductionist scientific approach, we overlook the fact that cause and effect cannot be worked out in any detail. The number of variables affecting any given situation in life is so many and so unpredictable that there is no such thing as scientific certainty. It is more sensible, Peat argues, to begin with a holistic view which seeks meaning in the conjunctions and patterns of existence. Common-sense experience of cause and effect is only one limited way of understanding the world.

In any case, the insistence on scientific thinking contradicts a lot of what analysts actually do. Whatever our theoretical orientation we tend to agree that the totality of the experience of the session is of basic importance. I shall quote Anthony Storr on this point, from an essay on psychoanalysis and creativity:

> If Freud had been able to accept that play, fantasy and dreaming were attempts to come to terms with, and master, reality rather than to escape from it, he would not have had to lay down his arms before the problem of the creative artist nor have felt that the grandest creations of art were unsolved riddles to his understanding . . . Art and science are both concerned with

seeking order in complexity and unity in diversity. (Storr, 1985, p. 168)

In other words, Freud tried and failed to confine his theory to a scientific account of mental life, believing that fantasy had to be given up in the adaptation to external reality; whereas Jung was always aware of the value of the non-rational. There is plenty of evidence from Freud's letters and conversations that he did not succeed in convincing himself of the scientific nature of psychoanalysis. In terms of Bohm's theory, Freud equated reality with explicate order, while Jung was aware of the wider reality or implicate order. Scientifically-minded people are guilty of a category error if they think that the value of psychoanalysis can be attributed to its status as a science.

As psychoanalysts we have a special insight into the interplay of the rational and irrational in mental life which can contribute to the evolving paradigm. The holistic view of mind as information implies that the way the mind works is ultimately the way the world is. The Western view of science and reality assumes cause and effect and linear time in a way that is unknown in other parts of the world. Freud seems to have been aware of this; for example, he suggested to Einstein, in their correspondence about war, that Einstein's physics was just as much a myth as his own theory (Freud, 1933). It seems that the psychoanalytic movement, rather than Freud himself, created the myth that psychoanalysis is a mechanistic, reductionist science. In particular, it was Strachey's conscious intention, in translating Freud into English, to use the language of science. Despite the many virtues of the *Standard Edition*, the use of this text as the definitive version of Freud has meant that the imaginative and creative qualities of Freud's prose have been submerged.

Jung's insistence on the integrity of the personality and the search for wholeness is increasingly attractive as the times change. His interest in alchemy, once derided by rationalists, makes better sense in the context of the ending of scientific certainty. The idea of alchemy as bad chemistry did not hinder Jung in his understanding of the symbolism of psychic transformations. Further, the notion of the collective unconscious is widely accepted outside psychoanalytic circles. Jung amassed evidence for the existence of recurring myths in different cultures, which demonstrate the workings of similar unconscious forces in different times and places. This cannot be proved scientifically, but it is absurd to disregard the manifestations of innate patterns of thinking because they are unscientific.

I will just quote one famous example (Jung, 1927). When Jung was a young psychiatrist he saw a paranoid-schizophrenic patient squinting at the sun and moving his head from side to side. The patient told him the sun had a penis, which moved from side to side to create the wind. Four years later Jung came across an ancient Greek text about a Mithraic liturgy. It described a vision in which a tube was hanging from the disc of the sun. If the tube was to the east there would be a west wind; if the tube was in the west, an east wind would blow. Jung went on to point out that in some mediaeval paintings of the Immaculate Conception a tube reaches down from Heaven through which the Holy Ghost descended. The Holy Ghost was originally thought of as a rushing wind.

It was perfectly feasible to dismiss this kind of evidence forty or even twenty years ago, but nowadays it looks rather different. Heisenberg argued that ultimate reality is not to be found in electrons, mesons and protons but in something that lies beyond them, in abstract symmetries which manifest themselves in the material world and which could be taken as the scientific descendants of Plato's forms. These symmetries can be thought of as having an immanent and formative role that is responsible for the material forms of nature. The concept of archetypal symmetries which can manifest themselves in the human mind is just one of many possible ways of stating this idea.

Theories are emerging from many different disciplines which treat mind and information as identical. I shall give two examples. The first is the new science of Chaos, which gives mathematical expression to the patterns of natural forms and events (Gleick, 1987). Similar patterns, of unimaginable complexity, have been demonstrated in widely differing situations, from turbulence in liquids to the irregularity of coastlines, the unpredictability of the weather, and fluctuations in the stock markets. Fractal geometry, the mathematical basis of Chaos, has flourished with the development of computers, which can demonstrate how these patterns recur no matter how many times they are magnified.

The most striking example is the Mandelbrot set, which is illustrated in Gleick's book by a series of photographs of increasing magnification. From the beginning to the end of the series the magnification is × 1 million, with the same motifs repeating within each other on a smaller scale as the magnification increases. Each element in the pattern is part of the grand design, and at the same time there is a universe within each grain of sand which can be revealed by magnifying the pattern. Looking outwards, the single element could be said to represent the infinitesimal smallness of a human being in the cosmos. Looking inwards, it can be a representation of the infinite complexity of the human mind. My personal response to this book is to imagine that the patterns of Chaos could provide a way of describing the repetition compulsion. Compulsive behaviour follows a recognizable pattern, and yet each repetition is in a different context, from which it cannot be isolated. Is it possible that the rhythms of near-repetition in the patterns of Chaos could describe such behaviour? It is even possible that the study of these natural rhythms could reveal the innate patterns of mental activity.

The second example is the Gaia hypothesis, James Lovelock's concept of the world as a self-regulating organism (Lovelock, 1982). Lovelock is an eclectic scientist and enormously creative. He has invented instruments to test his own and other people's theories, including some for space research. His theory is simultaneously scientific and holistic. Previous theories of life have held that plants and animals evolve on, and are distinct from, the earth as an inanimate planet. Lovelock has shown, through experiments of his own devising, that all living things are part of one great organism evolving over the span of geological time. This theory has provided a focus for many holistic ideas, particularly environmental ones. It points to the need for a new paradigm and it is also compatible with Bohm's theory of implicate order.

I cannot mention Lovelock without touching on the psychology of creativity. Lovelock's immensely fertile mind is largely geared to solving practical problems, yet he must be using primary process to a large degree to conceptualize possible solutions. He exemplifies Sylvano Arieti's idea that we need the notion of a tertiary mental process to describe the successful combination of primary and secondary process in adults (Arieti, 1976). This holistic concept would surely include the capacity to play with ideas.

If one accepts that there is an ordering intelligence informing the natural world, it follows that it is manifested in physical and psychological ways. Jung's concept of the collective unconscious is that it contains information which has never previously been conscious in the mind of the individual, in contrast to Freud's view. Now that the controversy between the two men is long dead, surely it is sensible to accept both theories.

The physicist Wolfgang Pauli, Jung's analysand and collaborator, was struck by the connection between psychology and physics. Jung and Pauli wrote that the physicist's investigation of matter and the psychologist's exploration of mind were different ways of approaching the same underlying reality (Jung and Pauli, 1955). Perhaps mind and body are simply different aspects of a single reality viewed through different frames of reference (Storr, 1987, p. 204).

Science changed, through quantum mechanics, from being impersonal to having to include the observer in the experiment. Paradoxically, the supposedly personal nature of the mind was changed by Jung's work to include a deep impersonal layer. Meaning is the kernel both of material structures and the collective unconscious. This meaning is at the heart of the 'objective intelligence', that formative generative principle which is neither matter nor mind. This repeats Bateson's idea that mind is immanent in all living things. Bohm goes even further in his idea that everything is enfolded in the totality or holomovement so that the distinction between animate and inanimate matter only exists in the explicate order of science and common sense. I find these ideas helpful in thinking about what really goes on in the process of psychoanalysis.

The progress of science produces ever-increasing specialization and fragmentation which results in patterns of meaning being lost. This is a major problem in the world today which causes many people to reject science. In terms of yin and yang, Western society is heavily overloaded with masculine yang values. A holistic world view would restore the balance of masculine and feminine. Science does not address, let alone solve, the human problems of existence and it explicitly repudiates value judgements. In psychoanalysis this way of thinking has led to one of the worst muddles in the profession – the idea that anything less than five, or perhaps four, sessions per week is not proper analysis. The lack of consensus about the actual figure reveals its absurdity. This doctrine has persisted without regard to changing circumstances or the increasing length of treatment. We have ended up with a quantitative criterion of excellence, and no sign of a qualitative way of differentiating psychoanalysis from psychotherapy. This is the result of a supposedly value-free attitude; in practice it imposes hidden values on the patient. If patients are allowed to decide the frequency of their sessions, a more spontaneous and potentially creative situation is established. The same thinking applies to fees. If the patient participates in a discussion to agree the appropriate fee, many of the negative effects of an imposed fee and imposed rules can be avoided.

Now I shall give some examples of recent theoretical papers by members of the Independent Group which seem to me to be holistic in outlook. Perhaps the most important holistic thinker is Winnicott. His view of mental health as the capacity for illusion, the rejection of too much sanity, and the need for some non-integration is a holistic and non-scientific view of analysis which has become implicit in Independent Group thinking. His concept of true and false self introduced a qualitative distinction between authentic and inauthentic behaviour which embodies Langer's belief that a meaningful existence is essential for mental health.

Nina Coltart's paper 'Slouching towards Bethlehem' was a personal statement of a holistic point of view which has been widely influential (Coltart, 1985). In 1990 she gave a lecture on 'Attention' in which she compared the quality of attention required of the analyst with the kind of attention that leads to enlightenment in Buddhist meditation. She quoted a passage by a Western Buddhist monk which could be taken without alteration as a description of the analytic attitude.

Dennis Duncan's paper 'The feel of the session' was about the quality of empathy (Duncan, 1990). He has also written about the changing paradigm in the British Psycho-Analytical Society. Michael Parsons explored the similarities of psychoanalytic technique and the martial arts of the Far East (Parsons, 1984). He wrote of psychoanalysis as a way of being, and of the necessity for constant regrounding in technique and basic principles in order to maintain this position. This paper illustrates in clinical terms a view earlier expressed by Karl Pribram:

> We need not polarize as opposites the hard-headed analysis and the search for structures (in the brain) and the wonder and awe when we view the embodiment of these structures. Those most productive of scientific fact have maintained, throughout a lifetime of contribution, just these spiritual qualities and as scientists they are ready and capable to defend spirit as data. This is science as it was originally conceived: the pursuit of understanding. (Pribram, 1976)

In his appreciation of Marion Milner, Parsons summarizes her work as follows: 'Her books are investigations of a state of mind which allows a deeper awareness of the truth precisely by giving up the assumptions of knowledge and opening one's vision as widely as possible to the unlooked-for and the unthought-of' (Parsons, 1990, p. 423).

Another influential author who has no roots in science is Christopher Bollas. His work is concerned with the patient's individual idiom and the possibility of shaping one's own destiny through insight instead of being governed by blind fate (Bollas 1987, 1989). Although his approach is quite different, he has some similarities with Jung. I could mention many others, and there is no particular significance in my selection.

There is a vast difference between analysts with the outlook which I am calling holistic and those analysts who believe that psychoanalytic theory can be thought of as a set of scientific formulations. Analysts who think scientifically believe that everything is essentially knowable, an attitude which fosters self-aggrandizement. Perhaps it is the prerogative of the Independent Group to keep in mind just how little we know or can know.

I have used Jung as a symbol of a holistic world view which includes spiritual values. We need a comparable symbol for psychoanalysis to express the spiritual qualities in our understanding of Freud, which has been overshadowed by the idealization of him as a scientist, and which has involved clinging to an outmoded concept of science. The change in attitude which I am advocating would answer many of the criticisms of psychoanalysis as unscientific. It is only with an outdated notion of science that psychoanalysis is devalued for not being something which it should not claim to be.

As the millennium approaches we can anticipate another psychological revolution comparable to the birth of psychoanalysis at the end of the last century. My hope is that as we witness the disintegration of the old order, the phoenix arising will take the form of a holistic paradigm.

REFERENCES

Arden, M. (1984) 'Infinite sets and double binds', *Int. J. Psycho-Anal.* 65: 443–52.
—— (1985) 'Psychoanalysis and survival', *Int. J. Psycho-Anal.* 66: 471–80.
—— (1987) 'A concept of femininity', *Int. Rev. Psycho-Anal.* 14: 237–44.
Arieti, S. (1976) *Creativity: The Magic Synthesis.* New York: Basic.
Bateson, G. (1980) *Mind and Nature.* London: Fontana.
Bohm, D. (1980) *Wholeness and the Implicate Order.* London: Routledge & Kegan Paul.
Bollas, C. (1987) *The Shadow of the Object.* London: Free Association Books.
—— (1989) *Forces of Destiny.* London: Free Association Books.
Coltart, N. (1985) 'Slouching towards Bethlehem . . .', in G. Kohon, ed. *The British School of Psychoanalysis: The Independent Tradition.* London: Free Association Books, 1986, pp. 185–99. Reprinted in *Slouching Towards Bethlehem . . . And*

Further Psychoanalytic Explorations. London: Free Association Books, 1992, pp. 1–14.

—— (1990) 'Attention', *British J. Psychotherapy* 7: 164–74. Reprinted in *Slouching Towards Bethlehem . . . And Further Psychoanalytic Explorations*. London: Free Association Books, 1992, pp. 176–93.

Duncan, D. (1990) 'The feel of the session', *Psychoanalysis and Contemporary Thought* 13: 3–22.

Freud, S. and Breuer, J. (1893) *Studies in Hysteria*, in James Strachey, ed. *The Standard Edition of the Complete Psychological Works of Sigmund Freud*, 24 vols. London: Hogarth, 1953–73, vol. 2.

Freud, S. (1933) 'Why war?' S.E. 22, pp. 195–215.

Gleick, J. (1987) *Chaos*. Cardinal.

Jung, C.G. (1927) 'The structure of the psyche', in *Collected Works* vol 8. Reprinted in A. Storr, ed. *Jung: Selected Writings*. Fontana Pocket Readers, 1983, pp. 66–8.

Jung, C.G. and Pauli, W. (1955) 'The interpretation of nature and the psyche'. Reprinted in A. Storr, ed. *Jung: Selected Writings*. Fontana Pocket Readers, 1983, pp. 336–9.

Kuhn, T. (1962) *The Structure of Scientific Revolutions*. Chicago, IL: Chicago University Press.

Langer, S. (1942) *Philosophy in a New Key*. London: Oxford University Press. Reprinted Harvard Paperbacks, 1978.

Lovelock, J. (1982) *Gaia: A New Look at Life on Earth*. Oxford: Oxford University Press.

Parsons, M. (1984) 'Psychoanalysis as vocation and martial art', *Int. Rev. Psycho-Anal.* 11: 453–62.

—— (1990) 'Marion Milner's "Answering Activity" and the question of psychoanalytic creativity', *Int. Rev. Psycho-Anal.* 17: 413–24.

Peat, F.D. (1988) *Synchronicities*. New York: Bantam.

Pribram, K. (1976) 'Transcendentalism and the logical paradox', in G.G. Globus and others, eds *Consciousness and the Brain*. New York: Plenum Press.

Rycroft, C. (1956) 'The nature of the analyst's communication to the patient', *Int. J. Psycho-Anal.* 37: 469–72. Reprinted in *Imagination and Reality*. London: Hogarth, 1968.

Storr, A. (1985) 'Psychoanalysis and creativity', in P. Horden, ed. *Psychoanalysis and the Humanities*. London: Duckworth. Reprinted in *Churchill's Black Dog*. London: Collins.

—— (1987) 'Jung's conception of personality', in A. Peacocke and G. Gillett, eds *Persons and Personality*. Oxford: Blackwell.

Zinkin, L. (1984) 'The hologram as a model for analytical psychology', *Journal of Analytical Psychology* 32: 1–21.

Address for correspondence: 16 Dealtry Road, London SW15 6NL, UK

PUBLICATIONS RECEIVED AND NOTICED

All books are published in London unless otherwise stated.

C. Fred Alford, *The Psychoanalytic Theory of Greek Tragedy*, Yale University Press, 1993, 218 pages, hb £18.50.

Lou Cannon, *President Reagan: The Role of a Lifetime*, Touchstone/Simon & Schuster, 1992, 948 pages, pb £10.99.

Dorothy W. Cantor (ed.), *Women as Therapists: A Multitheoretical Casebook*, New Jersey: Jason Aronson Inc., 1992, 264 pages, pb $21.00.

Cornelius Castoriadis, *Philosophy, Politics, Autonomy: Essays in Political Philosophy*, Oxford: Oxford University Press, 1992, 304 pages, pb £12.95.

Michel de Certeau, *The Writing of History*, New York: Columbia University Press, 1991, 370 pages, pb $18.00.

Delia Cushway and Robyn Sewell, *Counselling with Dreams and Nightmares*, Sage Publications, 1992, 141 pages, pb £9.95.

Windy Dryden (ed.), *Hard-Earned Lessons from Counselling in Action*, Sage Publications, 1992, 140 pages, pb £8.95.

R.V. Fitzgerald, *Conversations in Psychotherapy: Ways of Working with Individuals, Couples and Families*, New Jersey: Jason Aronson Inc., 1992, 384 pages, hb $37.50.

David S. Freeman, *Family Therapy with Couples: The Family-of-Origin Approach*, New Jersey: Jason Aronson Inc., 1992, 416 pages, hb $40.00.

E. Gaddini, edited by Adam Limentani, *A Psychoanalytic Theory of Infantile Experience: Conceptual and Clinical Reflections*, Routledge: The New Library of Psychoanalysis, 1992, 220 pages, pb.

Emanuel E. Garcia, *Understanding Freud: The Man and His Ideas*, New York and London: New York University Press, 1992, 174 pages, hb.

Anthony Giddens, *The Transformation of Intimacy: Sexuality, Love and Eroticism in Modern Societies*, Cambridge: Polity Press, 1992, 212 pages, hb £19.50.

Sander Gilman, *The Jew's Body*, Routledge, 1992, 303 pages, pb £10.99.

Leon Grinberg, *Guilt and Depression*, Karnac Books, 1992, 336 pages, pb £19.95.

Peter Heller, *Anna Freud's Letters to Eva Rosenfeld*, Madison: International Universities Press, 1992, 210 pages, hb $30.00.

Jeremy Holmes, *Between Art and Science: Essays in Psychotherapy and Psychiatry*, Routledge, 1992, 227 pages, pb £14.99.

Robert Langs, *Science, Systems, and Psychoanalysis*, Karnac Books, 1992, 287 pages, pb £18.95.

Beryce W. MacLennan and Kathryn R. Dies, *Group Counselling and Psychotherapy with Adolescents*, New York: Columbia University Press, 1992, 282 pages, hb $34.50.

Philip Manfield, *Split Self/Split Object: Understanding and Treating Borderline Narcissistic and Schizoid Disorders*, New Jersey: Jason Aronson Inc., 1992, 384 pages, hb $47.50.

Gael Elton Mayo, *Living with Beelzebub*, Quartet Books, 1992, 146 pages, hb £12.95.

Luciana Nissim Momigliano, *Continuity and Change in Psychoanalysis: Letters from Milan*, Karnac Books, 1992, 184 pages, pb £15.95.

Luciana Nissim Momigliano and Andreina Robutti, *Shared Experience: The Psychoanalytic Dialogue*, Karnac Books, 1992, 270 pages, pb £18.95.

Jerome Neu (ed.), *The Cambridge Companion to Freud*, Cambridge: Cambridge University Press, 1992, 356 pages, pb £12.95.

Charlotte Krause Prozan, *Feminist Psychoanalytic Psychotherapy*, New Jersey: Jason Aronson Inc., 1992, 384 pages, hb $50.00.

Robert S. Segal (selected and introduced by), *The Gnostic Jung: Including 'Seven Sermons to the Dead'*, Routledge, 1992, 259 pages, pb £9.99.

Laurence Spurling (ed.), *From the Words of My Mouth: Tradition in Psychotherapy*, Routledge, 1992, 165 pages, pb £12.99.

Louis H. Stewart, *Changemakers: A Jungian Perspective on Sibling Position and the Family Atmosphere*, Routledge, 203 pages, pb £12.99.

P.F. Strawson, *Analysis and Metaphysics: An Introduction to Philosophy*, Oxford: Oxford University Press, 1992, 144 pages, pb £7.95.

Frances Tustin, *Autistic States in Children*, revised edition, Routledge, 1992, 255 pages, pb.

C. Philip Wilson, Charles C. Hogan, Ira L. Mintz (eds), *Psychodynamic Technique in the Treatment of the Eating Disorders*, New Jersey: Jason Aronson Inc., 1992, 440 pages, hb $50.00.

Elizabeth Wright (ed.), *Feminism and Psychoanalysis: A Critical Dictionary*, Oxford: Basil Blackwell, 1992, 485 pages, pb £16.95.

CONTRIBUTORS TO THIS ISSUE

Margaret Arden worked in the National Health Service during the 1950s as an adult psychiatrist, and during the 1970s in child and adolescent psychiatry. In private practice as a psychoanalyst for the last fifteen years, she has published several theoretical papers which have in common the theme of changing paradigms in psychoanalysis.

Helmut Dahmer is a founder member of the Hamburg Institute for Social Research, and Professor at the University of Darmstadt.

Anthony Elliott is Research Fellow in the Department of Political Science, University of Melbourne, Australia. He is author of *Social Theory and Psychoanalysis in Transition: Self and Society from Freud to Kristeva* (Blackwell, 1992), *Critical Psychoanalytic Theory: An Introduction* (Blackwell, 1993), and, with Stephen Frosh, editor of *Psychoanalysis and Cultural Studies: The Debate over General Theory* (Routledge, forthcoming).

Karl Figlio is a psychoanalytic psychotherapist, an Associate Member of the Association for Group and Individual Psychotherapy, and a Fellow of the Department of Sociology, University of Essex. He has been active in the professionalization of psychotherapy, and has sat on the Council of the UK Standing Conference for Psychotherapy.

Michael Fordham is a Training Analyst of the Society of Analytical Psychology, and co-editor of the *Collected Works of C.G. Jung*. He is the author of several books and of numerous papers in scientific journals.

Evelyn Heintges is a graduate student at the Centre for Psychoanalytic Studies at the University of Kent, Canterbury.

David Mayers is a psychotherapist in private practice. He is a Member of the Council of the London Centre for Psychotherapy, and Clinical Liaison Co-ordinator, Centre for Psychoanalytic Studies at the University of Kent, Canterbury.

Renos Papadopoulos PhD is a training analyst for the Independent Group of Analytical Psychologists, and a Consultant Clinical Psychologist at the Tavistock Clinic, London. He has edited *Jung in Modern Perspective* (Wildwood House, 1984; Prism Press, 1991), and the four-volume work *C.G. Jung: Critical Assessments* (Routledge, 1992). He is the editor of *Harvest: Journal for Jungian Studies*.

Andrew Samuels is a Training Analyst of the Society of Analytical Psychology, and a Scientific Associate of the American Academy of Psychoanalysis. His books include *Jung and the Post-Jungians* and *The Plural Psyche*. His next book, *The Political Psyche*, is published in 1993 by Routledge.

Sonu Shamdasani lectures in psychology at the College of North-East London, and is Consultant to the Psychoanalytic Forum of the Institute of Contemporary Arts, London. He is the editor of a collection of essays on philosophy and psychoanalysis (Routledge, forthcoming).

Martin Stanton is Director of the Centre for Psychoanalytic Studies at the University of Kent, Canterbury, and author of *Sandor Ferenczi: Reconsidering Active Intervention* (Free Association Books, 1991).

NOTES TO CONTRIBUTORS

The editors encourage critical thinking within the analytical tradition, broadly conceived. They hope to stimulate the discussion of theory, practice, institutionalization and training in psychoanalysis, psychotherapy and related areas, including their historical, social and political aspects; and of psychoanalytic – including group-analytic – understanding of social, cultural and political processes.

The Editor and Managing Editor invite articles, commentaries, reflective pieces on training and work, letters, brief notes on publications and diary items. They also welcome consultation at an early stage of thinking or writing, as well as suggestions for contributions.

Manuscripts and enquiries should be sent to *Free Associations*, 26 Freegrove Road, London N72RQ. Manuscipts must be in triplicate, double spaced throughout, with wide margins. Authors must also supply a reasonably accurate word count with their submission.

References should be cited in the text (Smith, 1988, pp. 1–10) and listed alphabetically at the end of the article: Smith A (1988) 'A contribition on style', in E. Smith, ed. *Contributions on Style*. Colchester: Jay, 1989; or Smith, A. (1988) *A Contribution on Style*. Colchester: Jay. A style sheet is available.

Free Association Books holds the copyright of contributions published in *Free Associations*, unless otherwise arranged and indicated. Final versions of manuscripts undergo minimal copy-editing in preparation for publication, and, to avoid delay, authors are not sent a copy-edited text unless they specifically requested it. Authors do receive proofs and are asked to correct them, but additional changes to the text at this stage must be minimal and at the author's expense.

Please feel free to contact the Editor or Managing Editor at any time about a proposed contribution or a contribution in production.

JOURNAL
OF THE
BRITISH ASSOCIATION
OF PSYCHOTHERAPISTS

Number 24   January 1993

The British Association of Psychotherapists is a professional organis-
ation, founded in 1951, which offers academic courses in analytical
psychotherapy. The Journal publishes contributions to the theory and
practice of analytical psychotherapy and articles concerning the application of these concepts.

The current issue includes:

CHARLES RYCROFT	Further thoughts on symbolism
GORDON HARRIS	Projective identification from a Jungian perspective
JUDY COOPER	Different ways of structuring the frame: according to Winnicott, Khan and Langs
SIMON ARCHER	Shame, guilt and counterfeiting
ELIZABETH MACLAY	A patient has a hysterectomy: the implications following abuse in childhood
GERALDINE GODSIL McGUIGAN	Infant observation

BOOK REVIEWS and OBITUARIES

Please send £6.00 – which includes postage and packing – to: Adminis-
trative Secretary, B.A.P., 37 Mapesbury Road, London NW2 4HJ

EDITORIAL BOARD: Midge Stumpfl (Editor); Helen Alfillé (Book
reviews); Jane Pettit

Manuscripts should be sent to: The Editors, 21 Cantelowes Road,
London NW1 9XR

Books for review should be sent to: Helen Alfillé, 25 Elgin Crescent,
London W11 2JD

_____**Artesian Books**

Publishers of The British Journal of Psychotherapy

BRITISH JOURNAL OF PSYCHOTHERAPY

Editor: Dr R D Hinshelwood
St Bernard's Hospital, Southall, Middlesex, England.

This journal takes articles on clinical and theoretical topics relevant to the psychotherapist practising privately or in institutions. The emphasis is on papers which concern the practice of ANALYTICAL PSYCHOTHERAPY; or which concern the APPLICATION of psychotherapeutic practice and theory to institutions, society and other settings.

The profession of psychotherapy is splintered by internal divisions. This Journal is intended as a forum for a discussion and debate, for the profession as a whole. It has the backing of the majority of the analytically orientated psychotherapy organisations but it is not solely aligned with any one of them.

SUBSCRIPTIONS Volume 9 (Autumn '92–Summer '93): £21 for individuals, £42 to libraries and institutions (outside UK £27 and £48). Order from: **Artesian Books, 18 Artesian Road, London W2**

MANUSCRIPTS: 5 copies of manuscripts, with references in the style of the Journal, should be submitted to the Editor.

FA^B

Forthcoming from FREE ASSOCIATION BOOKS

SCHIZOPHRENIA
AND HUMAN VALUE

BY PETER BARHAM

Schizophrenia is a serious illness but it need not be an incapacitating one. Our present understanding of it is in part the heritage of nineteenth-century thought, yet it is also fused with our contemporary understanding of the social world. Peter Barham approaches the difficult problem of characterizing schizophrenia via an account of the institutional and intellectual contexts that gave rise to its formulation as a chronic condition. More than this, however, in his exploration of the relation of schizophrenia to moral community, he enlarges our understanding of rationality itself.

£14.95
ISBN 1 85343 196 6

PRE-PUBLICATION ORDERS FOR
SCHIZOPHRENIA AND HUMAN VALUE
SHOULD BE SENT DIRECT TO FREE ASSOCIATION BOOKS
26 FREEGROVE ROAD LONDON N79RQ

FORTHCOMING FROM
FREE ASSOCIATION BOOKS

LOVE OF BEGINNINGS
by J.-B. Pontalis
Translated by James Greene with Marie-Christine Réguis
Foreword by Adam Phillips

Winner of the Prix Femina Vacaresco and considered a masterpiece of autobiography, this is J.-B. Pontalis' lyrical meditation on his own life. One of France's pre-eminent psychoanalysts, co-author of the classic *The Language of Psychoanalysis*, he has also been a member of the editorial committee of *Les Temps Modernes*.

Love of Beginnings is a reverie on his personal trajectory and ponders especially his 'love and hatred of words' - language's limits and abuse and the imperialistic claims made on its behalf, in their different ways, by Sartre and Lacan. In the tradition of Montaigne, it is an essay that instantiates aspects of Pontalis' life, including his experience as a pupil of Sartre at a Paris lycée in 1941 and as a student of Lacan in 1954.

'Language . . . is the distant, insistent echo of all our losses'; 'language is separation'. *Love of Beginnings* is not a book for psychoanalytic specialists only. Rather than being about psychoanalysis, it exemplifies what psychoanalysis is about: passion, time and mourning, embedded in the flesh. Accessible, witty, profound, here thought is embodied, the word made carnal, and the author's losses become our own. Admiration for *Love of Beginnings* extends to these judgements: 'a perfect autobiography, bearing nothing superfluous'; 'a bold, exemplary, miraculous work'.

J.-B. Pontalis is a senior editor with France's most prestigious publisher, Gallimard. There he is General Editor of two series which he created, the literary series *L'Un et l'autre* and the psychoanalytical *Connaissance de l'inconscient*. He has written several books, translated in many countries: *Apres Freud, Frontiers in Psychoanalysis* (Hogarth Press), *Perdre de vue, La Force d'attraction*. He is also a full member and training analyst of the French Psychoanalytic Association.

192 pages   pb 1 85343 129 X   £12.95